HR Analytics: Fundamentals and Applications

Edited by

Sandeep Kumar Kautish

Apex Institute of Technology
Chandigarh University
Mohali, Punjab
India

&

Anuj Sheopuri

Department of Management
Harlal Institute of Management & Technology
Greater Noida
India

HR Analytics: Fundamentals and Applications

Editors: Sandeep Kumar Kautish and Anuj Sheopuri

ISBN (Online): 978-981-5274-19-6

ISBN (Print): 978-981-5274-20-2

ISBN (Paperback): 978-981-5274-21-9

need for a court order if at any point you breach any terms of this License Agreement. In no event will any delay or failure by Bentham Science Publishers in enforcing your compliance with this License Agreement constitute a waiver of any of its rights.

3. You acknowledge that you have read this License Agreement, and agree to be bound by its terms and conditions. To the extent that any other terms and conditions presented on any website of Bentham Science Publishers conflict with, or are inconsistent with, the terms and conditions set out in this License Agreement, you acknowledge that the terms and conditions set out in this License Agreement shall prevail.

Bentham Science Publishers Pte. Ltd.
80 Robinson Road #02-00
Singapore 068898
Singapore
Email: subscriptions@benthamscience.net

CONTENTS

FOREWORD i

PREFACE ii

LIST OF CONTRIBUTORS iii

CHAPTER 1 ROLE OF HR ANALYTICS IN PEOPLE MANAGEMENT: CHALLENGES AND OPPORTUNITIES IN THE INDIAN IT/ITES SPACE 1
Freeda Maria Swarna M., Shaheed Khan, Panch Ramalingam and *Amarnatha Reddy P.*
    INTRODUCTION 2
    HR ANALYTICS? 3
    HR ANALYTICS, PRACTICE, ADOPTION, IMPLEMENTATION, AND OUTCOME 8
        Objectives of the Research 9
        Methodology 9
        Sample Size 9
        Tool for Research 10
        Results, Discussion, and Conclusion 10
    IT COMPANIES OF INDIA AND THEIR CONTRIBUTION TO HR ANALYTICS 12
        TCS, HR Analytics 13
    INFOSYS HR ANALYTICS 13
        Indian IT Entities and Overseas Engagement and HR Analytics 14
        Global IT Majors and HR Analytics 15
        HR Teams, HR Analytics, and How the Business Sees the Scenario 15
    CONCLUSION AND THE WAY FORWARD 17
    CONSENT FOR PUBLICATION 21
    ACKNOWLEDGEMENTS 21
    REFERENCES 21

CHAPTER 2 IMPACT OF HR ANALYTICS ON ORGANIZATIONAL PERFORMANCE: A MODERN APPROACH IN HR 24
Nidhi Srivastava and *Isha Bhardwaj*
    INTRODUCTION 24
        Descriptive Analytics 26
        Diagnostic Analytics 26
        Predictive Analytics 27
        Prescriptive Analytics 27
        Human Resource Analytics (HR Analytics) 27
        Benefits of HR Analytics 28
        Organizational Performance Metrics 28
            Productivity 28
            Organizational Effectiveness 29
            Industry Ranking 29
        Proposed Conceptual Model 30
            Hypothesis (1a) 30
            Hypothesis (1b) 30
        Objectives of the Study 31
    METHODOLOGY 31
        Secondary Data Analysis 31
            Google 31
            Microsoft 32

HP	32
IBM	33
Unilever	34
Literature Review	34
Global Perspectives on HR Analytics	36
North America	36
Europe	37
Asia-Pacific	37
Organizational Performance	37
The Influence of HR Analytics as a Mediator of Organizational Performance within The Context of Human Capital Management	38
Implications of the Study	39
DISCUSSION AND CONCLUSION	39
REFERENCES	40
CHAPTER 3 PREDICTIVE ANALYTICS IN RECRUITMENT AND SELECTION PRACTICES	42
Sasirekha V., Nithyashree N. and Sarulatha N.	
INTRODUCTION	42
Understanding HR Analytics in Recruitment and Selection	44
Data Collection	44
Candidate Sourcing	44
Predictive Analytics	44
Employee Retention	44
Diversity and Inclusion	44
Candidate Assessment	45
Employee Retention	45
Continuous Improvement	45
Importance of Recruitment and Selection	45
Data-Driven Decision Making	45
Cost Management	45
Strategic Work Force Planning	46
Enhancing Candidate Experience	46
Compliance and Legal Considerations	46
Key Aspects of Recruitment and Selection in HR Analytics	46
Job Analysis	46
Sourcing	47
Screening	47
Interviewing	47
Assessment	47
Background Checks	47
Reference Checks	47
Decision Making	47
Offer and Negotiation	47
Onboarding	47
Legal Compliance	48
Diversity and Inclusion	48
Feedback and Improvement	48
Employer Branding	48
Technology Integration	48
Candidate Experience	48

Methods of Recruitment and Selection in HR Analytics 48
   Job Posting and Job Boards 48
   Social Media Recruitment 49
   Employee Referrals 49
   Recruitment Agencies 49
   Predictive Hiring Models 49
   Behavioral Assessments 49
   Video Interviews 49
   Resume Screening 49
   Talent Pipelining 49
   Diversity Hiring 49
   Candidate Experience Analysis 50
   Time-to-Fill and Cost-Per-Hire Analysis 50
   Exit Interviewing Analysis 50
Implementation of HR Analytics in Recruitment And Selection 50
   Define Objective 50
   Data Collection 50
   Data Integration 50
   Data Cleaning 50
   Data Analysis 51
   Choose Analytics Tools 51
   Identify Key Metrics 51
   Identify Improvement Areas 51
   Continuous Monitoring 51
   Feedback Loop 51
   Actionable Insights 51
   A/B Testing 51
   Training 52
   Reporting 52
   Iterative and Improve 52
Key Indicators of Recruitment and Selection in HR Analytics 52
   Time to Hire 52
   Quality of Hire 52
   Applicant-To-Interview Ratio 53
   Interview-To-Offer Ratio 53
   Time spent in each hiring stage 53
Future Trends 53
   Predictive Analytics 54
   AI-Powered Automation 54
   Real-Time Data Analysis 54
   Video and Social Media Analytics 54
   Integrated HR Technology Platforms 54
CONCLUSION 54
REFERENCES 55
CHAPTER 4 HR ANALYTICS AND PEOPLE MANAGEMENT 57
Sasirekha V., Abinash T. and *Venkateswara Prasad B.*
INTRODUCTION 57
Understanding HR Analytics 59
   Descriptive Analytics 59
   Diagnostic Analytics 59

      Predictive Analytics 59
      Prescriptive Analytics 59
   The Importance of People Management 60
      Talent as a Competitive Advantage 60
      Employee Productivity 61
      Employee Retention 61
      Adaptability to Change 61
      Employee Experience 61
   Integration of Hr Analytics 62
      Optimizing Talent Acquisition 62
      Enhancing Performance Management 62
      Workforce Planning and Succession Management 63
      Employee Participation and Preservation 63
      Strategic Decision-Making 63
   Metrics and Key Performance Indicators (KPIs) In People Management 64
      Talent Acquisition Metrics 64
      Employee Engagement and Satisfaction Metrics 65
      Performance Management Metrics 65
      Training and Development Metrics 65
      Diversity and Inclusion Metrics 66
   Implementing HR Analytics in Organizations 66
      Leadership Buy-In 66
      Data Infrastructure 67
      Data Governance 67
      Skills and Training 67
      Identify Key Metrics 67
      Select Analytics Tools 67
CASE STUDIES 67
   Case Study 1: Google Inc. 67
   Case Study 2: IBM 68
   Case Study 3: Hilton Worldwide 68
FUTURE TRENDS IN HR ANALYTICS 69
   AI and Machine Learning Integration 69
   Predictive Workforce Analytics 69
   Employee Experience Enhancement 69
   Real-time Data Analytics 69
   Ethical and Responsible AI 69
   People Analytics Centers of Excellence 70
   Employee Well-being Metrics 70
   Continuous Learning and Upskilling 70
CONCLUSION 70
REFERENCES 71

CHAPTER 5 UNLEASHING THE POWER OF HR ANALYTICS: ENHANCING PEOPLE MANAGEMENT STRATEGIES 72
   Parulkumari Bhati
   INTRODUCTION TO HR ANALYTICS AND ITS SIGNIFICANCE IN MODERN BUSINESS 72
   Defining HR Analytics 73
   The Power of Data-Driven Insights 73
   The Significance in Modern Business 73

Informed Decision-Making 73
Enhanced Recruitment 73
Employee Retention and Engagement 73
Performance Optimization 74
Strategic Workforce Planning 74
Personalized Learning and Development 74
Ethical and Inclusive Practices 74
The Transformation from Traditional HR Practices to Data-Driven Decision-Making 74
From Paper to Pixels: Digitalization of HR Records 75
The Emergence of HR Metrics and Reporting 75
Transition to Predictive Analytics 75
From Intuition to Evidence-Based Insights 75
Enhanced Recruitment Strategies 75
Tailored Learning and Development 75
Proactive Employee Retention 76
Strategic Workforce Planning 76
Ethical and Inclusive Practices 76
Enhancing People Management Strategies through HR Analytics 76
Informed Recruitment and Selection 76
Precise Employee Onboarding 77
Employee Engagement and Retention 77
Personalized Learning and Development 77
Optimized Performance Management 77
Effective Team Composition 77
Proactive Succession Planning 77
Workforce Diversity and Inclusion 78
Strategic Workforce Planning 78
UNDERSTANDING HR ANALYTICS 78
Core Components of HR Analytics 79
Data Collection and Integration 79
Data Cleaning and Preprocessing 79
Descriptive Analytics 79
Diagnostic Analytics 79
Predictive Analytics 79
Prescriptive Analytics 79
Data Visualization and Reporting 80
Ethical Considerations 80
Continuous Improvement 80
The Process to Collect - HR-Related Data 80
Data Collection 80
Data Preparation and Cleaning 81
Data Analysis 82
Interpretation of Insights 82
Communication 83
Continuous Improvement 83
THE ROLE OF DATA-DRIVEN INSIGHTS IN STRATEGIC DECISION-MAKING 83
Informed Decision-Making 84
Evidence-Based Strategy Formulation 84
Mitigating Risk 84
Objective Evaluation 84
Measurable Impact 84

Flexibility and Agility 85
Alignment with Organizational Goals 85
Enhancing Employee Experience 85
BENEFITS OF HR ANALYTICS FOR PEOPLE MANAGEMENT 85
Informed Decision-Making 86
Enhanced Recruitment Strategies 86
Improved Employee Retention 86
Personalized Learning and Development 86
Performance Optimization 86
Strategic Workforce Planning 86
Employee Engagement Enhancement 86
Objective Diversity and Inclusion Initiatives 87
Effective Succession Planning 87
Measurable Return on Investment (ROI) 87
Data-Driven Culture 87
Continuous Improvement 87
APPLICATION OF HR ANALYTICS IN PEOPLE MANAGEMENT 87
Recruitment and Talent Acquisition 88
Sourcing Optimization 88
Candidate Success Prediction 88
Cultural Fit Assessment 88
Employee Onboarding and Integration 88
Onboarding Effectiveness 88
Time to Productivity 88
Performance Management 88
Objective Performance Evaluations 88
Performance Trends 88
Learning and Development 89
Skill Gap Identification 89
Learning Impact 89
Employee Engagement and Retention 89
Engagement Insights 89
Attrition Risk Prediction 89
Team Dynamics and Collaboration 89
Team Composition 89
Collaboration Patterns 89
Compensation and Benefits 89
Fair Compensation 89
Benefit Preferences 89
Succession Planning 90
High-Potential Identification 90
Leadership Development 90
Diversity and Inclusion 90
Representation Analysis 90
Inclusion Initiatives 90
Exit and Turnover Analysis 90
Turnover Causes 90
Cost of Turnover 90
Workforce Planning 90
Future Skill Demands 90
Talent Supply Forecasting 91

ETHICAL CONSIDERATIONS IN HR ANALYTICS 91
   Data Privacy and Consent 91
      Informed Consent & Data Security 91
   Transparency 91
      Clear Communication 91
   Fairness and Non-Discrimination 92
      Avoiding Bias 92
      Equal Treatment 92
   Anonymization and De-Identification 92
      Protecting Privacy 92
   Accountability and Ownership 92
      Ownership of Data 92
      Accountability 92
   Use Limitations 92
      Scope of Use 92
   Employee Empowerment 93
      Access to Data 93
   Continuous Monitoring and Auditing 93
      Ethical Review 93
      Adjustments 93
   Cultural and Social Sensitivity 93
      Respecting Diversity 93
   Compliance with Regulations 93
      Legal Frameworks 93
CHALLENGES AND FUTURE TRENDS 94
   Challenges 94
      Data Quality and Integration 94
      Data Privacy and Ethics 94
      Skill Gap and Talent Shortage 94
      Resistance to Change 95
      Bias and Fairness 95
      Technology and Infrastructure 95
   Future Trends 95
      Predictive and Prescriptive Analytics 95
      AI and Machine Learning 95
      Employee Experience Analytics 96
      Workforce Planning for Remote and Hybrid Work 96
      Emotional and Sentiment Analysis 96
      Real-Time Analytics 96
      Natural Language Processing (NLP) 96
      Integration with HR Technology 96
      Ethical AI and Responsible Analytics 97
      Skill Development for HR Analytics 97
  CONCLUSION 97
  REFERENCES 98

CHAPTER 6 PREDICTING EMPLOYEE PERFORMANCE USING PREDICTIVE MODELS 100
  Sasirekha V., Gomuprakash P. and *Suresh R.*
  INTRODUCTION 100
   Key Components of Predicting Employee Performance 101
      Data Collection and Preparation 102

Feature Selection and Engineering 102
Model Selection 102
Model Training 102
Validation and Evaluation 102
Feature Importance Analysis 102
Model Interpretability 102
Deployment and Monitoring 103
Ethical Considerations 103
Iterative Improvement 103
The Importance of Predictive Employee Performance 103
Informed Decision-Making 103
Talent Acquisition 103
Resource Allocation 104
Strategic Workforce Planning 104
Personalized Development 104
Employee Engagement 104
Retention Strategies 104
Performance Metrics Alignment 104
Reduced Turnover Costs 104
Effective Succession Planning 105
Integration of Predicting Employee Performance and Predictive Models 105
Data Collection and Management 105
Model Development and Validation 105
Integration into HR Processes 105
Talent Acquisition and Recruitment 106
Performance Management 106
Succession Planning 106
Employee Development 106
Retention Strategies 106
Continuous Improvement 106
Leadership Support and Training 106
Ethical Considerations 107
Communication and Transparency 107
Implementing Predictive Employee Performance in an Organization 107
Define Objectives and Goals 107
Assemble a Cross-Functional Team 107
Data Gathering and Preparation 107
Choose Predictive Models 107
CASE STUDIES 108
Case Study 1 108
Tech Startup Talent Optimization 108
Case Study 2 108
Retail Chain Employee Succession Planning 108
Case Study 3 109
Financial Services Performance Enhancement 109
CONCLUSION 109
REFERENCES 110

CHAPTER 7 A NUMBERS GAME OR A PEOPLE GAME: AN ANALYTICAL APPROACH
TO BRING THE BEST TALENT TO THE ORGANIZATIONS 112
Rupa Rathee and Madhvi Lamba

INTRODUCTION 112

HR ANALYTICS 114

SPHERES OF IMPLICATIONS OF ANALYTICS IN HR 116

TALENT MANAGEMENT 116

    Talent Management Analytics 118

    Recruitment 118

    Recruitment Metrics 119

        Applicants Per Opening 119

        Application Completion Rate 119

        Candidate Call-back Rate 120

        Source of Hire 121

        Time to Fill 122

        Time to Hire 123

        Selection Ratio 123

        Quality of Hire 124

        Cost Per Hire 125

        Offer Acceptance Rate 126

        Recruitment Funnel Effectiveness 126

        Sourcing Channel Effectiveness 127

        Sourcing Channel costs 127

        Recruiter Performance Metrics 128

        Candidate Experience 128

        Hiring Manager Satisfaction 128

        Retention Rate 128

        Attrition Rate 128

    How Talent Management Analytics can Help in People Management? 130

CONCLUSION 131

REFERENCES 131

CHAPTER 8 HR ANALYTICS: CONCEPT, ADVANTAGES AND OBSTACLES 133

Jatinder Kaur and *Srijan Gupta*

INTRODUCTION 134

    Concept of HR Analytics 134

    Literature Review 134

    Research Methodology 136

    Secondary Data 136

    Purposes of the Study 136

    Types of HR Analytics 137

        Descriptive Analytics 137

        Diagnostic Analytics 137

        Predictive Analytics 138

        Prescriptive Analytics 138

    HR Analytics Tools 138

        R - Programming 138

        Excel 139

        Tableau 139

        Python 139

        Power BI 139

        Visier 139

    Benefits of HR Analytics 140

        Lower Employee Turnover 140

Making the Hiring Process More Effective 140
Improving Training 140
Effective Hiring 140
Gaining Additional Employee Insights 140
Supporting Increased Productivity at Work 140
Metrics Monitored by HR Analytics 141
Efficiency of Training 141
Risk to Human Capital 141
Offer Acceptance Rate 141
Absenteeism 141
Employee Training Expenses 141
Revenue Per Employee 142
Obstacles to Implementing HR Analytics 142
Data Quality Challenge 142
Data Governance Issue 142
Deficiency in Data Analysis Skills 142
Insufficient IT Resources 143
Diverse Data Landscape 143
Employee Resistance 143
CONCLUSION 143
REFERENCES 144
SUBJECT INDEX 145

FOREWORD

HR analytics sometimes goes by other names like people analytics, talent analytics, workforce analytics, and human capital analytics. It is defined as the analytics of human resources (employees), which includes the entire life cycle of employees, such as hiring, engaging, and ultimately, retention. HR has been undergoing a digital transformation for some time. With so much data, there has been a huge increase in the availability of unnecessary data, too. With so much ample data, it poses a challenge for HR professionals to sort and select the required data. Hence, HR practitioners must be able to read and understand HR analytics to create value for their organizations, as well as to improve their own capabilities. The tools and techniques will make sense of all of this information so one can make better HR business decisions. HR analytics empowers HR managers to be conversant with the idiosyncrasy of teams, which may be built upon people at multi-location workplaces. HR analytics is used for corporate decision making, achieving strategic goals, and sustaining a competitive advantage. The people-related data is procured, analyzed, and interpreted for the purpose of improvement. HRM focuses on supporting employees; people analytics brings science into HR. People analytics allows HR to quantify its efforts and impact in order to encourage better people decisions. It is the revival of people-driven scientific management.

In this foreword, I will focus primarily on the broader trend to think more analytically about almost everything and what that means for HR. This edited book provides a vital tool for HR practitioners to get familiar with the fundamentals of HR analytics, which is now a important for every HR professional. Actually, understanding and applying the data and analyzing it to solve real-life HR challenges is the main skill that has to be developed and enhanced. Today, there is no industry or field that is not using analytics. HR analytics has the potential to play a key role in the transformation process (*e.g.*, choosing and validating selection tools) that helps in decision making, *etc*. I wholeheartedly recommend this book for all who are grappling with how to capitalize on HR analytics and add greater value, as this book contains contributions by various professionals that make us understand effective HR practices. This book has an easy-to-understand format to illustrate the use of analytics to solve challenging problems that are commonplace in organizations.

Ali Wagdy Mohamed
Operations Research Department
Faculty of Graduate Studies for Statistical Research
Cairo University, Giza-12613, Egypt

PREFACE

This book, "HR Analytics: Fundamentals and Applications", aims to compile innovative methods and literature related to HR analytics. It throws light on the role of analytics in the human resource industry, portrays the challenges and resistance that are faced in the industry, and determines how HR analytics is transforming and supporting various activities in the field of HR. In recent decades, advances in information technology and systems have reduced the time HR professionals spend on transactional and administrative activities, thereby creating more time and opportunities for transformational activities supporting the realization of strategic organizational objectives.

The content presented in this book offers a variety of methods/techniques that will provide an effective and sustainable solution for analytics, which has turned out to be one of the most gripping and useful tools. Therefore, HR analytics can go a long way toward sensitizing people toward building upon employee relations. It helps to create an employee-centric organization by providing HR professionals the required skills and opportunities to work and adapt to a data-driven environment and make informed and data-backed decisions. The topics covered are – the roles of HR analytics in people management, how various tools and techniques are used in recruitment and selection practices, and also its role in predicting employee performance. Overall, the concepts, advantages, and obstacles of HR analytics are discussed.

This edited book sheds light on upcoming trends, challenges, and future research directions in HR analytics. The editors have explored the topics and the subjects that are impressive and impactful. We hope the exploration of what it takes to successfully launch and grow these capabilities will boost awareness of how HR professionals can lead the charge to change while elevating the function's status in the eyes of stakeholders.

We would like to express our heartfelt gratitude to our reviewers who have helped despite their hectic schedules. Thank you very much to all our authors for submitting their work. We would like to express our heartfelt gratitude to Bentham Science Publishers for accepting our proposal to edit this book and for their unwavering support throughout the editing process. Thank you to everyone who has contributed, directly or indirectly, to the completion of this edited book.

We believe the efforts we rendered for editing the book are worthwhile only if this book is of any use to the ordinary end-users of our society. This gratification will motivate us to produce more edited publications that will benefit society.

Sandeep Kumar Kautish
Apex Institute of Technology
Chandigarh University
Mohali, Punjab, India

&

Anuj Sheopuri
Department of Management
Harlal Institute of Management & Technology
Greater Noida, India

List of Contributors

Amarnatha Reddy P.	Custard Apple Consulting, Hyderabad, India
Abinash T.	Sri Sairam Engineering College, Chennai, India
Freeda Maria Swarna M.	Dharthi NGO, Bangalore, India
Gomuprakash P.	Sri Sairam Engineering College, Chennai, India
Isha Bhardwaj	IMS - Ghaziabad (University Courses Campus), Dehli, India
Jatinder Kaur	Rukmini Devi Institute of Advanced Studies, Affilated to GGSIPU, New Delhi, India
Madhvi Lamba	Department of Management Studies, Deenbandhu Chhotu Ram University of Science and Technology, Murthal, Haryana, 131039, India
Nidhi Srivastava	IMS - Ghaziabad (University Courses Campus), Dehli, India
Nithyashree N.	Sri Sairam Engineering College, Chennai, India
Panch Ramalingam	UGC-HRDC, Pondicherry University, Pondicherry, India
Parulkumari Bhati	Department of Humanities and Social Science, Institute of Technology, Nirma University, Gujarat, India
Rupa Rathee	Deenbandhu Chhotu Ram University of Science and Technology, Murthal, Haryana, India
Shaheed Khan	Research and Training, Dharthi NGO, Bangalore, India
Sasirekha V.	Faculty of Management, SRM Institute of Science & Technology, Vadapalani, Chennai, India
Sarulatha N.	Management Studies DG Vaishnava College, Chennai, India
Suresh R.	Management Studies, Sri Sairam Engineering College, Chennai, India
Srijan Gupta	Rukmini Devi Institute of Advanced Studies, Affilated to GGSIPU, New Delhi, India
Venkateswara Prasad B.	Management Studies, Sri Sairam Engineering College, Chennai, India

Role of HR Analytics in People Management: Challenges and Opportunities in the Indian IT/ITeS Space

Freeda Maria Swarna M.[1], Shaheed Khan[2,*], Panch Ramalingam[3] and **Amarnatha Reddy P.[4]**

[1] *Dharthi NGO, Bangalore, India*

[2] *Research and Training, Dharthi NGO, Bangalore, India*

[3] *UGC-HRDC, Pondicherry University, Pondicherry, India*

[4] *Custard Apple Consulting, Hyderabad, India*

Abstract: Human capability and capacity are what determine what an organization can do, and thence, managing human resources (HR), or human capital, is one of the most important, if not significant, functions of an organization. Considering the size of the organization, and in a day and age where organizations have thousands of employees that are spread across a wide geographical area, HR analytics comes into play. HR analytics, in a true sense, provides the necessary scientific support to decision-making and process improvement concerning a firm/organization's HR and the organization in general. The way organizations are growing, and the dynamic role that the HR ecosystem plays makes it pertinent that a robust HR analytics system is in place. With more organizations realizing that qualitative data helps to hire, engage, and retain the right talent, the investment in HR analytics has seen an increase. It is right to say that HR analytics aims to provide insights into how best to manage employees and reach business goals. Because of data availability, it is important for HR teams to identify data relevance and its usage, leading to maximizing return on investment (RoI). The chapter places a perspective on how HR is i) identifying high-performing applicants, ii) supporting the analysis of pertinent aspects of engagement, iii) identifying high-value career paths and leadership applicants, iv) analyzing strengths of prospective and existing associates, v) ushering in a qualitative and metric oriented performance management system (PMS), and vi) managing/predicting attrition.

Keywords: Data, HR analytics, Leadership, Performance management systems (PMS), Prediction, RoI.

---

* **Corresponding author Shaheed Khan:** Research and Training, Dharthi NGO, Bangalore, India;
E-mail: shaheeddharthi@gmail.com

Sandeep Kumar Kautish & Anuj Sheopuri (Eds.)

INTRODUCTION

Human resources (HR) analytics bridges the gap between HR activities in the corporate world and displays the outcomes that the decision makers receive from the same. With the Information Technology (IT) and Information Technology-enabled Services (ITeS) sector being considered the vibrant and dynamic segments for the innovative working culture, it is by choice that HR analytics plays a role that is unique and important, if not critical, to the HR function and the organization for ensuring decisions to be taken on a real-time basis.

The National Association of Software Companies (NASSCOM) stated that, "investing for growth is the primary focus of the Software business. One must realise that, (i) the forward-looking policies of the sector, (ii) a strong facet of governance, (iii) investment on talent, that is the crux of the industry, and (iv) digital trust, which makes efforts to ensure, privacy, security, and reliability across the spectrum; the IT/ITeS space in India is galloping toward a growth factor of $500 by 2030 (NASSCOM, 2023)." This is an incredible statement by Debjani Ghosh, President (NASSCOM, 2023), NASSCOM (https://nasscom.in), on the IT/ITeS and the way it is growing.

The IT/ITeS business segment, with its vast global delivery model (GDM) and enormous human capital for managing the onsite, offshore, nearshore, and even client locations, provides a huge opportunity for the human resources (HR) department to ensure the best for the organizations. HR engages itself in talent acquisition (TA), talent engagement (TE), talent management (TM), talent transformation (TR), and the various other activities to enable organizations to function smoothly. Sun (2022) put forward data about the totality of IT/ITeS employment for 2009-2022, which was enormous and stood at 4.85 million employees as of 2022 (Fig. **1**). This clearly sends a perspective that managing people, the most important facet of the business, must and should be done in a scientific way to ensure that the investment that is done in HR is captured well.

The sheer numbers clearly showcase the need for HR analytics, the metric that has become critical to the HR function. Bersin (2023) mentions the amount of data that is generated on account of the human capital that needs to be managed. Josh Bersin mentions that the single most common expenditure in most companies is people, followed by (i) salaries, (ii) benefits, (iii) real estate, and (iv) the domain of HR. The challenge is how do we manage this expenditure in the best way possible? Thence, the need of the hour is to 'integrate people data' (Bersin, 2023). It is here that Bersin (2023) introduces the facet of systemic people analytics (SPA), a new concept and a thought process about HR and the technologies it imbibes.

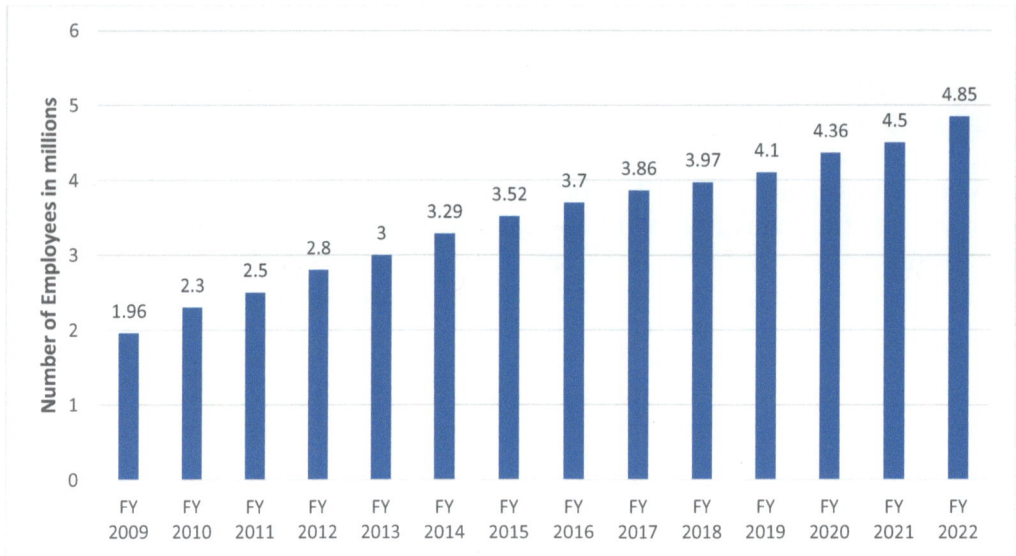

Fig. (1). Employment of IT/ITeS industry in India, 2009-2022, Sun (2022).

HR ANALYTICS?

For an HR professional or a layman, what is HR analytics? How does it impact the IT/ITeS sector in India? As mentioned by Chanakya Sehgal (Sehgal, 2023), a senior HR professional in the Indian IT Industry with nearly three decades of experience, "when HR analytics was spoken of, we thought, it just about numbers, about metrics, and what we need to put up to the leadership to decide. But as we progressed into understanding the dynamics of HR analytics, we realized that it was much more. HR analytics was an enablement to take decisions, decide, a course of action and ensure the same." Sehgal spoke of how academia has tried to define HR analytics, which fits the bill for the practitioner who would like the discipline to usher in positivity to the subject of human capital management. To enable the academic and the practitioner alike, HR analytics has been defined and considered a corporate practice by Marler and Boudreau (2017), wherein the enablement of IT uses (i) descriptive, (ii) visual, and (iii) statistical analysis of data and information related to human resources management (HRM) and its processes, human capital, organizational performance and, external economic benchmarks, which will establish and support business impacts and enable a data-driven decision-making system, which further helps the organization to move forward in a robust fashion. This provides a broad base to all those who are interested in HR analytics and furthers the cause of HR through the milestones provided in the seminal article by Coy (2017), which speaks of four levels/stages of workforce analytics, which was eloquently adapted by Banerjee (*et al.*, 2019), as seen in Fig. (**2**).

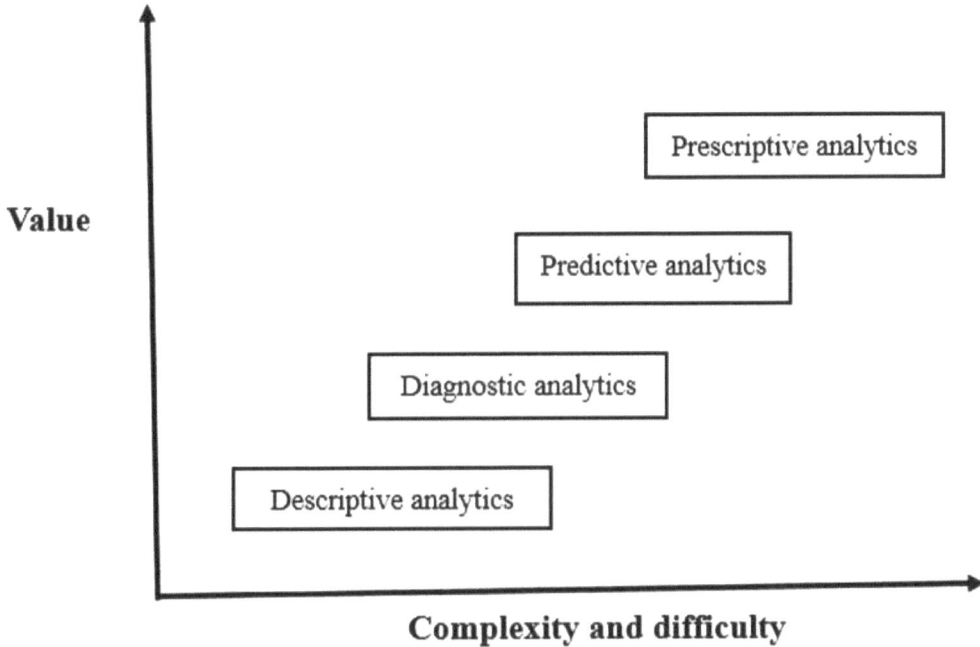

Fig. (2). The Four Stages of Workforce Analytics: What Level are you? (Banerjee *et al.*, 2019).

Speaking about four stages of workforce analytics, Academy to Innovate Human Resources (AIHR) (https://www.aihr.com) brought forth a clearer understanding of HR analytics, with Vulpen (n.d.) defining HR analytics as people analytics, workforce analytics, and talent analytics in a research paper on Network Perspective (https://www.networkpespective.io) (Network Perspective, n.d.). Besides, the domain of HR analytics focuses on (i) gathering, (ii) analyzing, and (iii) reporting HR data. This enables the organization to measure the impact of a range of HR metrics on the overall business performance and supports in considering decisions based on data available for internal and external operations. Therefore, HR analytics is a data-driven approach to qualitative HRM.

Heuvel and Bondarouk (2016), in their seminal research conducted at the University of Twente, Faculty of Behavioural, Management, and Social Sciences, the Netherlands (https://www.risutwente.nl), defines the subject of HR analytics as an area of study that stems from the systematic identification and systematic quantification of the people drivers of business outcomes, with the sole intent of making or considering better decisions. It is a belief, however, that the difference in labeling simply goes beyond the language, as HR analytics will make suggestions keeping in mind the responsibility of identifying and quantifying the people business drivers

The article also provides a qualitative understanding of the change that will engulf HR analytics over a ten-year period, which makes the understanding even clearer. The evolution leading to HR analytics is succinctly captured by Vupen (n.d.), who mentions that HR analytics and the subsequent decisions taken are no longer based on 'gut feeling' but follow a process as mentioned in the AIHR learning piece, which was inspired by the research work carried out at the Tilburg University (https://arno.uvt.nl). This research is articulated in Fig. (**3**) and provides for the evolution and the outreach to data-driven HR, which is the cornerstone of HR analytics as we see it today. Vupen (n.d.) also speaks about the fact that the revolution brought about by HR analytics ensures that HR departments do not just become a record room of data but use the data available at one's command to analyze, assess, and make decisions for the benefit of the corporation. HR department and the associates can make i) qualitative decisions based on data that is generated, ii) create a business case for interventions as required in the short and long term, iii) test the effectiveness of the interventions identified and arrived at, and iv) the domain/department of HR moving from being part of operations to a tactical partner and becoming a strategic partner. Furthering the case of the four stages of Coy (2017), Boatman (n.d.), in the article on AIHR, helped build (Fig. **4**), which, when juxtaposed with the thoughts of Banerjee (*et al.*, 2019), further provided a qualitative understanding of HR analytics.

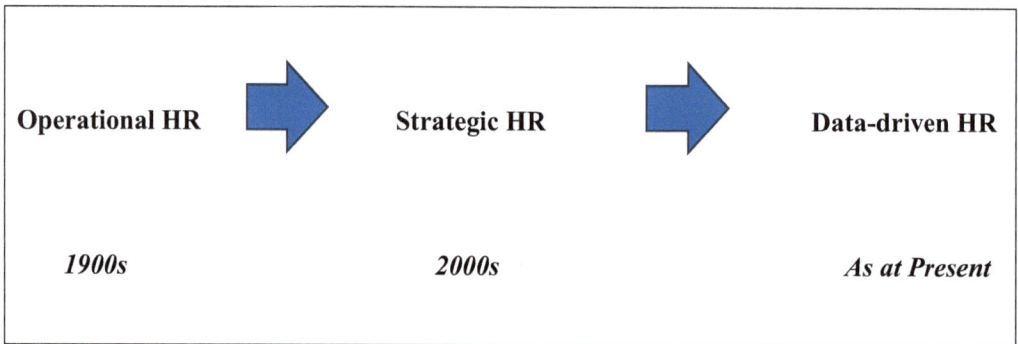

Fig. (3). The evolution of HR analytics (Vupen, n.d.).

Boatman (n.d.) put forward the nuances from a perspective of descriptive analytics, keeping in view certain questions. Why did it happen? with a focus on the diagnostic segment of analytics, what will happen? being in the domain of predictive analytics, and how can we make it happen? wherein the attribute is prescriptive. This clearly helps in establishing the cause for a through-put that will ultimately help HR in its outreach to the organization, with healthy people management practices and strategies and interventions that are distinct. If the academic world has defined the subject of HR analytics, it is worth seeing the tangent that comes about when the corporate defines the subject. Speaking of the fact that HR needs to up its people analytics skills, Oracle (2021), in its State of HR Analytics 2021 report, worked in tandem with the HR Research Institute (https://www.hr.com) and focused on people or talent analytics to collect, collate and analyze people related data for the purpose of producing inputs and interventions to the management and leadership and thereby support in improving decision-making. From a usage perspective, HR analytics generally includes the use of statistical methods, technologies, and expertise; besides, it also includes the facets of metrics and big data. This is a clear indication that corporations and the academia see eye to eye in regard to the HR analytics construct, which will help organizations benefit from inputs and throughputs that will support decision-making.

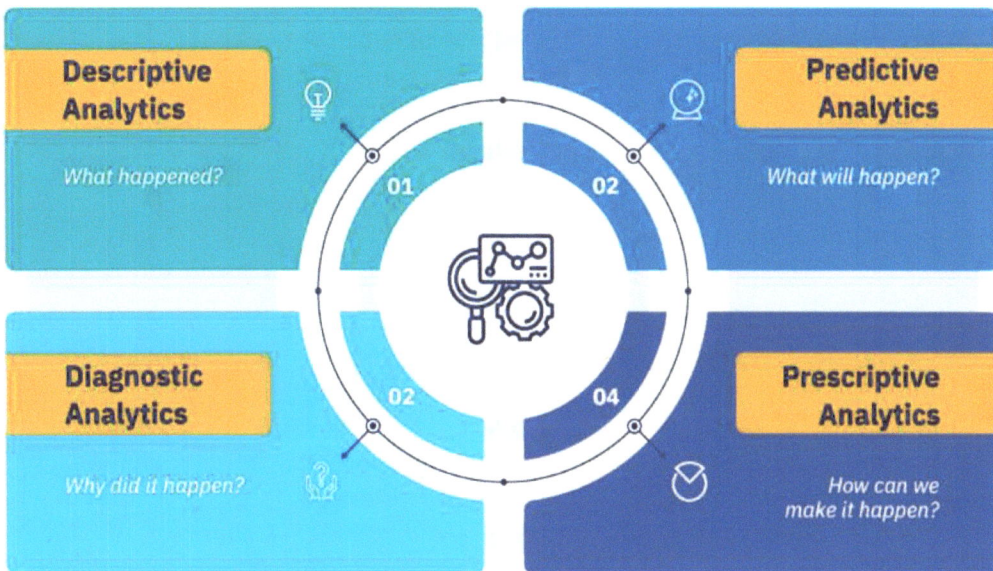

Fig. (4). The four types of HR analytics (Boatman, n.d.).

For every HR professional and student, Dave Ulrich offers words of wisdom that guide us to enable our views and apply these thoughts to the corporate and academia. Ulrich (1997), in *Human Resource Champions*, what many of us consider a bible in HR, articulates the thought that no one can predict, foresee, or envisage the future course for the HR profession. No one will be able to predict how HR practices and policies will change in the near and far future. One should not be fraught with obstacles but should think about the future, which will keep us in good stead and help us to prepare for the best. Thinking about the future will lead to innovative strategies and insights and help to change the existing HR practices. Speaking about analytics as a buzzword in HR, Ulrich (2022) mentions that analytics has become an important, if not critical, concept for the future of HR. He goes on to mention the four stages of the evolution of analytics, each with its own vocabulary (Fig. **5**), which will help in furthering the cause of catapulting HR and HRM to great heights and to get a seat in the corporate core.

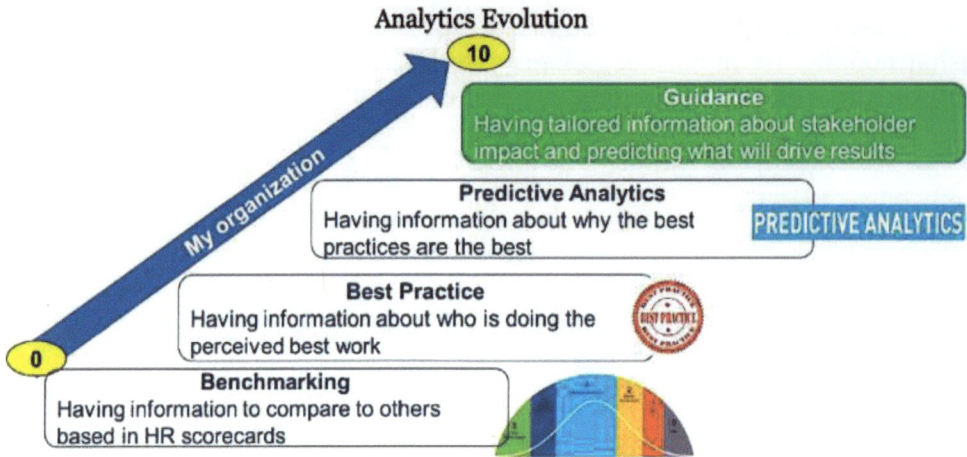

Fig. (5). Analytics Evolution (Ulrich, 2022).

The framework put forward by Ulrich (2022) clearly proposes the facets of benchmarking, best practices, predictive analytics, and guidance, suggesting the business and the corporate leadership a way forward. CV Sreekanth (Sreekanth, 2022), a mid-level HR Manager at L&T Infotech who is engagedin HR, mobility/immigration function, and compliance, mentions that HR analytics has helped to understand the way associates behave when it comes to the efficacy of compliance whilst they are onsite or near-shore. The tools of analytics adopted by an organization highlight data about any misfeasance that occurs on account of the actions of the employees, leading to a decision being taken that will ensure 'zero' or 'minimum' exposure. Ram Kiran Kanumuri (Kanumuri, 2023) is an HR professional who worked with two of the Tier 1 IT/ITeS companies of India and currently works in the Kingdom of Saudi Arabia with Mueen Human Resources Company (https://www.mueen.com.sa). He confirms that, with a large workforce, and most of them embedded with multiple clients and at multiple locations, it becomes pertinent that HR analytics is brought to the fore. The numbers that my organization engages are large considering the companies that we are engaged with, and maintaining and managing data about recruitment, performance appraisals, exits from projects and from the country, to salary and/or wage fixation are a challenge and it is analytics that is supporting my organization to ensure for the individuals and the organizations that we represent. This apart, the

Leadership team at Ms Mueen, take decisions based on the inputs analysed and also get a 'buy-in' *i.e.*, the concurrence of the client for the action to be taken. Ram Kiran Kanumuri also mentions that "in my two decades of experience as an HR professional, I got to speak in the initial days about HR being Strategic, today we speak about analytics as a tool that will help the organizations to move ahead, in fact, we in HR have started to assess, analyze and even predict, the way things will move, and this good for the organization and Team HR."

Ravi Ganti (Ganti, 2023), a people and compliance manager at Cognizant Technology Solutions (CTS) (https://cognizant.com), while mentioning an article that focused on the HR leader's ability to focus on 'identity', 'agility', and 'scalability' (Komm *et al.*, 2021), reveals that, "analytics in the HR business is very critical, and, post Covid-19 and the issues of Work from Home (WFH), Work from Anywhere (WFA) and now Work from Office (WFO), there was much confusion in data maintenance leading to an administrative fracture. The analytics and the related frameworks that were put in place, supported in arriving at decisions and ensuring an implementation of the mechanisms that the organization wanted to work along with." The thoughts put forward by Ravi Ganti clearly bring into discussion the facet of linking 'talent to value' that Komm (*et al.*, 2021) have articulated. He stated that the best talent would be shifted into critical value-driven roles (Scanlon, 2021) and the best people will be given important roles, as well as the organization will genuinely create value, as in the case of Tesla, which is an example of the effort to create a culture of a fast-moving innovative organization (Komm *et al.*, 2021). Komm (*et al.*, 2021) further add that to enable the transition, HR should manage talent in a dynamic way by building an analytics capability to mine data, which will further acquire human capital, and develop and retain the best talent. HR partners who articulate people's needs to the executive leadership, delivery ecosystem, and technology specialists by considering themselves as service providers ensure high returns on human capital investments. HR in general and business HR in particular need to engage the business, technology, and delivery leaders in a regular review of the associates. HR will be able to develop semi-automated and automated data dashboards that track the important metrics for critical roles and support decision-making.

HR ANALYTICS, PRACTICE, ADOPTION, IMPLEMENTATION, AND OUTCOME

Marler and Boudreau (2016), in well-received research, state that HR analytics is a practice that provides managers with information needed to link HR processes to employees' behaviors and ultimately to the outcomes and interventions that impact the organization and its effectiveness. Marler and Boudreau (2016) further state that successfully adopting HR analytics requires skilled personnel in the domain of analytics who will be part of the HR department as opposed to an individual or a group of analysts common to all functions of the organizations. Thus, HR teams need to further develop both their business and analytical skills to translate findings into solutions for improved business performance. It is, therefore, pertinent to note that HR analytics is not just a fancy term; it is a business, an important tool for evidence-based decision-making.

Satya Thopalli (Thopalli, 2023), an HR corporate leader with more than two decades of experience in the Indian IT sector and currently working with a global IT firm, mentions that people analytics or HR analytics is still evolving in the Indian scenario, as, in some cases, the organizations are not aware of what needs to be done; whereas global IT majors have a system in place that makes people analytics effective and important.

Objectives of the Research

The following were the major objectives of the research:

1. To discuss with HR leaders the impacts of HR analytics on their functioning.

2. To assess and analyze the collaboration of HR teams with the delivery units and their impact on the functioning of HR.

3. To get statements from the members of project management operations (PMO) about the utility of HR analytics.

Methodology

This study was conducted by using a semi-structured questionnaire, which was provided digitally. A total of two follows up were done by the authors with the prospective respondents. The researchers asked a total of 150 HR professionals to respond, of which a total of 139 responses were received, and 135 had no errors, which were finally considered for the analysis. The prospective respondents were asked two questions, which were adapted from an Oracle-sponsored State of HR Analytics study of 2021 (Oracle, 2021). The responses received were an eye-opener to the authors, which guided the reader to understand the efficacy of HR analytics.

Sample Size

The study was conducted by using random sampling on 150 HR associates in the IT sector. A total of 139 responses were received, and 135 responses, which did not have any errors, were considered for the analysis.

Tool for Research

The semi-structured questionnaire had two questions that were adapted from the State of HR Analytics Study by Oracle (Oracle, 2021).

Results, Discussion, and Conclusion

The data collected from the HR associates in the IT sector was analyzed and tabulated.

Fig. (**6**) provides a bird's eye-view picture of what the HR associates feel about HR analytics and how can analytics help usher in benefits for the organization. It is clear from the analysis of the responses received that the HR community

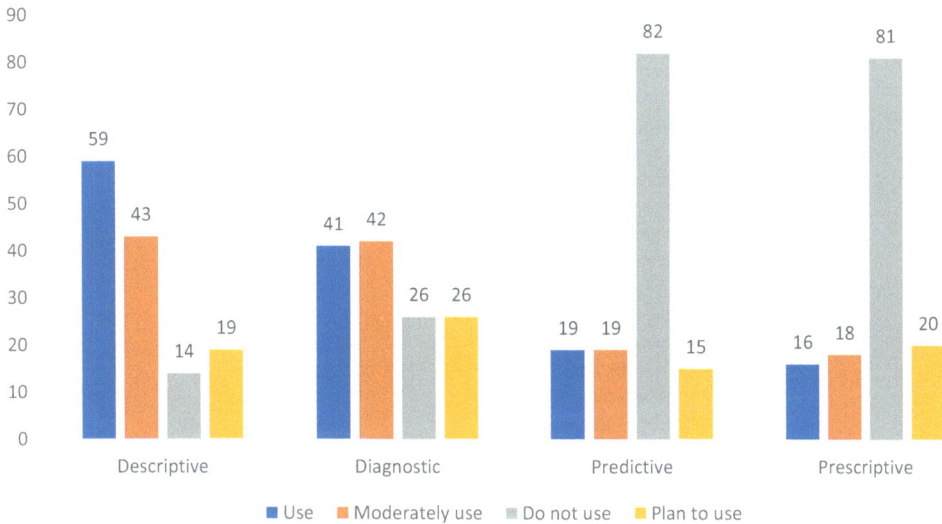

Fig. (6). The responses to questions on HR analytics four-stage framework.

has been using HR analytics tools to bring in a description of the issues being faced in the organization. Fifty nine of the respondents mentioned that they were using HR analytics and 43 stated that they were moderately using HR analytics, which was reasonable. However, by providing diagnostic solutions to the HR issues being faced in the organization, 41 of the 135 HR associates confirmed that they are providing diagnostic solutions in totality, and 42 mentioned that they were providing diagnostic solutions on a moderate basis but would start using the tools of HR analytics in its totality. The research, however, surprised the authors, as when it came to the predictive usage of HR analytics, 82 did not use it for predicting and/or for decision making, which meant that HR analytics was still finding a foothold in the IT/ITeS organizations. The framework of descriptive, diagnostic, and predictive leading to prescriptive measures is more of a lateral orientation, which will enable decision-making over a period. Eighty one of the 135 respondents stated that they did not use the data generated to suggest and prescribe solutions on the prescriptive platform to the business/delivery teams. This clearly meant that the HR associates were on the learning curve, and with more training and organizations mandatorily implementing HR analytics platforms, all four stages of HR analytics would be adhered to.

To the second question that the HR associates were queried upon, *i.e.*, the top five HR functional areas in HR that are unique to HR analytics, the following was the response (s) (Fig. **7**).

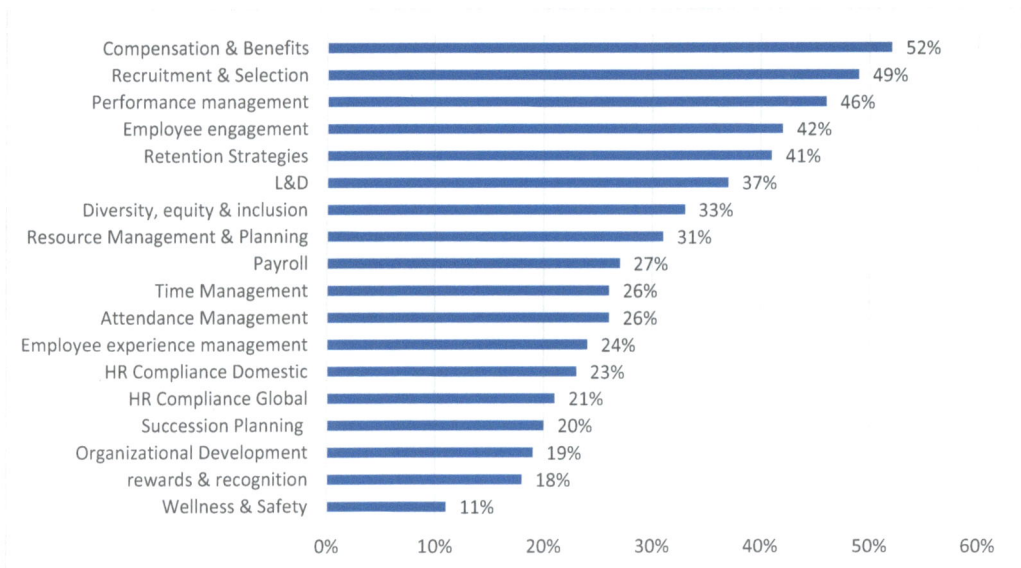

Fig. (7). Top five HR functional areas in HR that are unique to HR analytics.

The top five responses were:

- Compensation and Benefits (52%).
- Recruitment and Selection (49%).
- Performance Management (46%).
- Employee Engagement (42%).
- Retention Strategies (41%).

This, by and large, was not surprising, and Satya Thopalli (Thopalli, 2023), who had placed performance management as his number one variable, mentions, "Performance Management Systems (PMS) are a huge challenge to any HR and the organization/delivery ecosystem. With large teams in place for projects, a qualitative PMS system, which is metric oriented and helps in the analysis of each employee for his/her performance, which is documented, there will be far less controversies and even attrition that impacts on the projects."

The authors also looked at the bottom five and found some of the variables that were critical to the organization.

- HR Compliance (Global) (21%).
- Succession Planning (20%).
- Organizational Development (19%).
- Rewards and Recognition (18%).
- Wellness and Safety (11%).

The bottom five came as a surprise to the authors, who always believed that succession planning has been a challenge and will remain a challenge, though all agree that succession planning must be documented, as it will help with employee turnover and any other intervention that the HR and business teams would like to bring in.

IT COMPANIES OF INDIA AND THEIR CONTRIBUTION TO HR ANALYTICS

Indian IT companies, to ensure they can tackle the issues that they will face considering the ever-increasing human capital requirements, started working on systems that would capture the dynamics of HR metrics and analytics as well. As TV Sharma (Sharma, 2023), a Business HR partner with Coforge (https://www/coforge.com), responded in the discussion with the research team and mentioned, "even small IT companies like mine, have made efforts to ensure the dynamics of HR are captured well and we did go in for in-house systems that would capture all relevant aspects of the human capital. The larger IT companies too have shown the way to ensure HR analytics by developing programs not only for internal consumption, but for the customers as well and have offered solutions." Sharma further states, "we empower HR Employees with HR Analytics. This will have a significant impact on the HR team by providing data-driven insights and improving decision-making. It allows HR professionals to better understand trends in employee, performance, engagement, Compensation and Rewards. This information can and will lead to more effective talent acquisition, development, and retention strategies. HR Analytics can help streamline processes, optimise resource allocation, and enhance overall organisational goals achievement." The chapter tries to capture the way IT companies of India have made efforts to develop HR analytics solutions and investigates the efficacy of the same.

TCS, HR Analytics

Roy (2020), in a well-documented article in Tech Circle (https://www.techcircle.in), reported that Tata Consultancy Services (TCS) launched workforce analytics as a unified system of engagement that provides insights, foresight, and plans to enhance the productivity of the human capital and an experience to help organizations deal with talent management challenges. The development of an artificial intelligence-based human resource management system for employees, managers, and leadership within an enterprise lets an organization focus on workforce engagement through i) culture-based interventions, ii) occupational health and wellness, and iii) focus on making human resources skilled. Developed in the TCS Co-Innovation (COIN) (https://www.tcs.com/who-we-are/newsroom/tcs-in-the-news/tcs-cointm) center by a partner entity, dotin Inc, the management system supports in evaluating skills, recording personality traits and strengths, and learning the style of the associate and cultural compatibility, which augurs well for the organization that uses the resource management system. HR World (2020) reported that the resource management system would help in decision-making in the domain of a) leadership development, b) career management, and c) performance improvement facets of HR. The insights can then be used to match the right employee for the right role in the project, which will further help in putting high-performing teams together. The TCS (2020) media release also quoted Dinanath Kholkar (https://www.tcs.com), Global Head of Analytics and Insights of the company, who stated, "The new ways of working in today's corporate world, are fundamentally transforming the talent management function. One must note that, (i) role fitment, (ii) talent development and (iii) engagement can only be accomplished using available data, analytics, and cognitive technologies. Workforce Analytics at TCS has been designed to empower HR organizations with inputs that will help them deliver superior business outcomes and enhanced workforce experiences (www.tcs.com)."

INFOSYS HR ANALYTICS

Infosys People Analytics & Insights (https://www.infosys.com) launched the HR metric and dashboard solution system built on the Oracle HCM Cloud platform. This solution was designed to keep all the HR reporting needs across all the reporting groups in a single place. The manager (s) and business leaders, through the dashboard, get information and inputs of upcoming key events, by which they are able to manage the workforce and the organization to be compliant with the laws of the land. They can view analytics as it provides inputs on upcoming expirations of worker documents, probation, and contract end dates (Infosys, n.d.A). Another release of Infosys (n.d.B) provides information on the key features of the solution-providing platform, which creates many opportunities for customers who use robust systems, such as the one that has been created. Infotechlead (2023) reported that with robust systems in place, Aramco (https://www.aramco.com), a leading energy and chemical company, signed a memorandum of understanding (MoU) on the HR data and analytics that would enhance the employee experience through artificial intelligence, thereby improving the productivity of the associates.

Key features of Infosys HR analytics systems (https://www.infosys.com) (Infosys, n.d.B)

- Formulae-based scorecard for relevant HR key performance indicators (KPIs), which will enable the HR teams, along with the technology leadership and the project management operations (PMO), to formulate a strategy for corrective action.
- Logical grouping of HR metrics and KPIs within human capital management (HCM) systems.
- Ability to analyze data and display trends across business units, locations, departments.
- Compare the performance of various HR metrics with the internal targets at Infosys and industry benchmarks.

Indian IT Entities and Overseas Engagement and HR Analytics

A question that comes to mind is how are Indian IT companies adopting HR analytics in countries outside of India. Ram Kiran Kanumuri (Kanumuri, 2023) mentions, "Indian IT entities are functioning in Europe, USA, Japan, Singapore, Malaysia, and Australia-New Zealand for a long time now, besides the Middle East. They have adopted the nuances of HR analytics as required across the HR spectrum to ensure cohesion with the mother entities and the subsidiaries that spread all over the world. With good associate numbers in these countries, it is pertinent that HR analytics becomes a critical facet." Amarnatha Reddy (Reddy, 2023), a veteran in the IT/ITeS as a technology specialist and later as a subject management expert (SME) in HR, states, "when it comes to the emerging markets in the African continent and Latin America (LATAM), the Indian IT entities do face challenges, the number of employees either local or expatriates is small or the branches that the Indian entities have started is still small and growing. It is here that the usage of HR Analytics suffers. But over a period, the increase in projects and thereby the increase in local employment and even expatriate movements from across the world ensures an adherence of the HR analytics and benefits that one can accrue." A seasoned HR leader from a Tier 1 entity who wanted to remain anonymous, stated, "we find that in the IT entities of Indian origin and local entities in the African continent, in countries like, South Africa, Kenya, Tanzania, Ghana, and Nigeria, have adopted the norms of HR Analytics as the organizations grow. It can be seen in Nigeria wherein, the Pharmaceutical industry is large and the IT entities too work along on various paradigm adopting to the HR Analytics norms, which bring about an understanding that even the developing nations and the corporate entities within them, want to adopt the mechanisms of HR Analytics and benefit from them."

Global IT Majors and HR Analytics

Indian IT entities have gone miles ahead to ensure HR analytics comes to aid and supports the customers who use the platforms. The Global IT majors have also moved ahead and ensured platforms that will support and add value to the domain of HR analytics. The IBM Planning Analytics (https://www.ibm.com) (IBM, n.d.) has created a total solutions workforce planning analytics and reporting solution application, wherein automation and streamlining of HR management processes are done on one platform, which further help drive efficiency and agility in human capital management. As mentioned by an IBMer who wanted to remain anonymous, "the workforce planning software gives the user complete visibility into the existing workforce, the roadmap/path for jobs in the market, staffing metrics (existing and the pipeline requirement), besides the talent gaps that are to be found in the associates within the IBM system. The user (customer) will have a way to determine the best of action plans and cost-effective methods to acquire human capital, skill/reskill, train, and, ensure succession planning whilst ensuring an optimization of costs, increasing employee productivity, and reducing turnover *i.e.*, the attrition rate." This clearly means the IT world in India and the Global majors have ensured the best for themselves and the customers in the domain of HR analytics.

HR Teams, HR Analytics, and How the Business Sees the Scenario

HR is no doubt a support function in the IT/ITeS world. Human Resources Shared Services (HRSS) model makes the support that HR needs to provide even more challenging, for it is the experience that business and the delivery teams, who front end projects, derive, and generate the necessary business delight and/or associate/employee delight.

Collier and Schallenback (2017), in seminal research submitted to Cornell University (https://ecommons.cornell.edu/handle/1813/73716), opine that many organizations have adopted the HR framework referred to as the *three-legged stool* model that has within itself:

- Human Resources Business Partner (HRBP) ecosystem,
- Centres of Excellence (COE) and
- HRSS.

The constant evolution of HR operating models, HRSS, and HR operations has ensured the business takes in much of the transaction work and allows the COEs and HRBPs to focus on transactional work. Collier and Schallenback (2017) foresee three areas of evolution that will impact the HR ecosystem and the analytics domain, which in turn will impact the organization. The areas of evolution are:

- Overall construct of the HRSS Centre and the solution offerings,
- Focus on the objectives of the HRSS Centre, and
- The processes becoming mature with the advancement in technology.

With a construct of this kind, the role played by HR as part of the Global Business Services (GBS) (Collier and Schallenback, 2017), along with the dynamic HR analytics portfolio, is crucial if not critical. Many of decisions to be taken by HR are on the business side, which have an impact on the profit and loss and what is generically referred in the IT/ITeS world as 'bottom-line'.

The views of the delivery teams and primarily the PMO become pertinent asthey showcase the cause of HR and HR analytics. With more than a decade of experience in the IT space, Pritam Chakraborty, a PMO specialist at Wipro (https://www.wipro.com), mentions that, "HR analytics leverages data, data driven interventions to make informed decisions, improve processes (Singh, 2023), and enhances organizational efficiency in the areas of i) resourcing for a project; ii) the important aspect of Performance Appraisal and the fall-out, hitherto and more importantly; iii) Succession Planning in a project." Elaborating on the three facets and how HR and analytics play a role that will offset many calculations, Pritam mentions that, "HR analytics helps in augmenting a dashboard, that will predict the skills, the skill-sets and resources needed for a project, small or big. The analytics that HR provides helps in identifying the right employees with the necessary expertise and availability, optimizing resource allocation, and improving project success rates in the project (s)." It has been seen that some of the projects that the PMOs manage are large, with the onsite, near-shore, client location propositions adding to the challenges, and it is here that Pritam speaks of the fall-out of performance appraisal and how HR analytics will play a role in supporting PMOs and the delivery teams in making decisions. Pritam adds, "the insights that one gets into the performance of an employee by primarily analysing pertinent data points viz., productivity, the Key Result Areas (KRA), goals achieved, the feedback (at times from a 360° perspective) and with the analytics at hand, the appraisals become a) fair and objective and b) reducing the element of bias, that everyone speaks off. Moreover, the patterns of performance data, will help to predict potential performances issues that will lead to employee attrition/turnover; which known in advance, will help the PMO to plan and ensure 'zero gaps' on account of human capital." It is here that TV Sharma (Sharma, 2023), the Business HR Leader at Coforge (https://www/coforge.com), mentions, "Succession Planning is an issue, all the team members cannot be promoted in tandem, there will be star performers, who need to be taken care, and this needs to done with a metric oriented system, and it is HR analytics that adds value to the PMO and the delivery functions to decide based on the data opinions provided by HR." Pritam adds to the context of Succession Planning and states that, "HR analytics helps the PMO along with the HR teams who are integral part of the PMO, to analyse the associate skills, the experiences, and the career trajectories that the associates have identified, which enables them to be considered for future leadership roles in the projects and the organization." Therefore, the relevance of HR analytics is crystal clear for one to decipher.

CONCLUSION AND THE WAY FORWARD

HR analytics is here to stay. With a lot of changes happening in the corporate arena, the options of working from various locations, emerging challenges, teams not being able to meet on a regular basis,, and times when an employee must report to two managers or multiple stakeholders, analytics will surely play a valuable role in HR and the business ecosystem.

The research undertaken by the authors discussed the top five functional areas of HR as follows:

- Compensation and Benefits.
- Recruitment and Selection.
- Performance Management.
- Employee Engagement.
- Retention Strategies.

This clearly mean that the HR fraternity must engage itself to ensure the IT/ITeS business and the associates who are part of the delivery ecosystem. Representing the business ecosystem, Pritam has rightly stated, "PMS, and recruiting, it is the succession planning that one needs to work on, as if the issues faced are not addressed adequately, the only fall out will be employee turnover/attrition, which should be arrested at any given point in time, considering the project that any company will be working on." This does not come as a surprise, as succession planning was one of the bottom five components that were responded to. However, when one looks at the organizations on a real-time basis, succession planning has been considered the crux of the HR-related issues that HR, in a true fashion, must deliver. But it is an irony that the HR professionals chose to ignore the fact, though some (20% of the respondents) realized the importance and placed succession planning among the top five facets of HR analytics. But then, there is a lot to be done. Whether it is Tier 1 or Tier 2 IT companies, HR analytics will become a critical component to dabble with. Deepa (Deepa, 2023), Head of HR at Kloud9 (https://www.kloud9.nyc/), has rightly stated that, "HR analytics is the bread and butter for the HR professionals, it is the enter life cycle of the employees in a firm. It helps with recruitment to assess and access the market and ensure a qualitative talent market analysis, the salary ranges that one can offer in comparison to competition, the levels of attrition and if there is a need for discussions with the associates, PMS too is an important dimension that dots the HR spec." From Deepa's statement, it is very clear that HR analytics embraces the a-z of HR, from recruitment to the exit associate/employee concerned, which enables the organization to make informed decisions. A Vertical HR Head in Wipro (https://www.wipro.com), Meenal Gupta, mentions, "new age Analytics and AI tools are the key to managing talent Analytics, succession planning and predictive attrition at scale. Today's AI systems can analyse and integrate hundreds of millions of employee profiles and other HR data points to enable organisations to take more robust people decisions." This is a clear indication that HR analytics is here to stay and ensure for the fraternity of HR and the corporate world.

Whatever may be the top or bottom five components that the authors did their best to assess with the HR fraternity, India stands on top of the world when it comes to HR analytics. Referring to a Deloitte University Press report (https://www2.deloitte.com) (Fig. **8**), U-next (2020) reports that India is not just a stalwart supporter of HR analytics but a true pioneer in People Analytics in the Digital HR domain. Hence, as stated by TV Sharma (Sharma, 2023), "adequate training of the HR professionals will help in proliferation of the HR analytics dynamics, which further will become an important throughput for the organizations to focus on usage of HR analytics and the metrics that it will generate to help in decision-making."

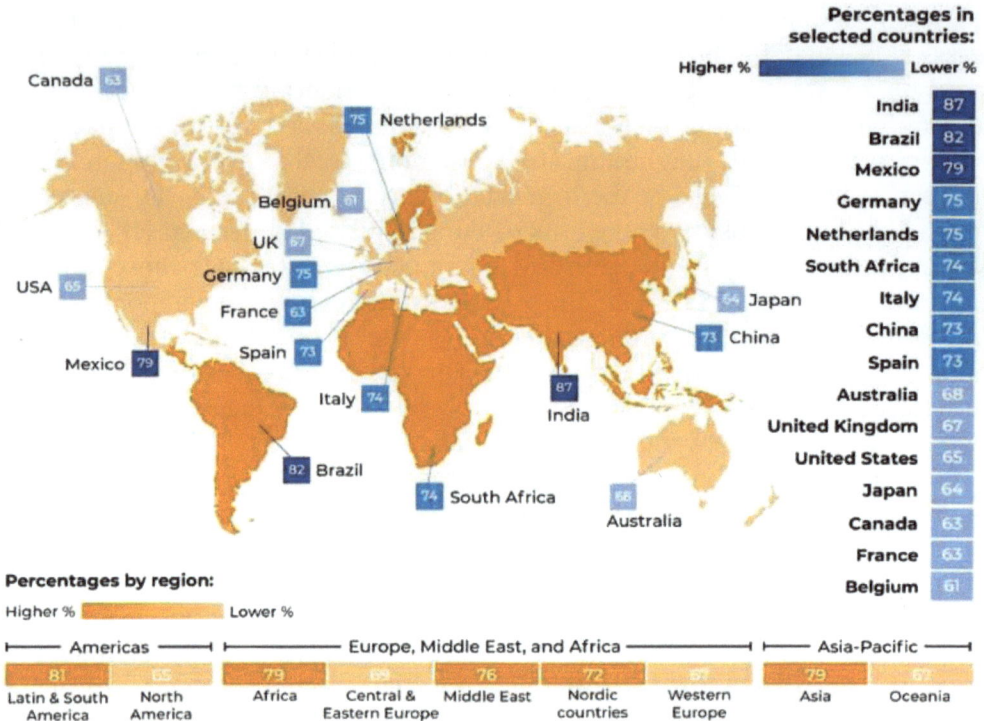

Fig. (8). Deloitte Survey Report (https://www2.deloitte.com) focusing on Digital HR: Percentage of respondents rating the trend important or very important (U-next 2020).

Pritam (2023), being part of the PMO, has been able to provide a right understanding of the way HR teams have been working with the business and delivery teams to deliver as required. Pritam mentions that, "though the HR team members in the PMO are keen to ensure a metric and data driven HR system, at times, because of the lack of training or even academic learning, the HR professionals are not able to deliver. However, a good number of HR team members, have been ramping up their skills to ensure for the business and provide accurate decision-making postulates, which will be the highlight of any HR analytics system."

People Data Labs (2022) discusses an article that helps the layman and the professional alike to understand the nuances of HR analytics and speak of the benefits and challenges that come about as one dwells in the domain. Fig. (**9**) emphatically informs the readers about the benefits that must be addressed. Whilst speaking of 'data consolidation', the research portrays the benefits that occur in the dimensions of:

Fig. (9). The benefits and challenges of using HR analytics to drive decisions (People Data Labs, 2022).

- Increased workforce productivity.
- Identification of skill gaps among the associates.
- Improvement in the employee experience.
- Staff retention ability.
- Improvement in talent acquisition.

However, as the business of HR and HR analytics deepens itself in the corporate world, the challenges also become unique.

- Consolidation of data from various departments/units and third-party resources.
- Challenges privacy and compliance of various hues.
- Insufficient IT resources for HR data analytics.
- Inability to access quality data.
- Data bias potential.

Despite the fact challenges that exist for HR analytics, it has become pertinent that organizations and the HR fraternity adopt the frameworks and measures put forward by HR analytics, which help organizations move toward a better decision-making entity.

CONSENT FOR PUBLICATION

The chapter has been researched with the intent to information and knowledge outreach to the academia and the corporate world of HR. The authors confirm the publication of the chapter in digital and print media and are hopeful that the research will benefit the stakeholders of the IT/ITeS world in India and the world.

ACKNOWLEDGEMENTS

The authors would like to thank all the respondents for their time for the research and their responses. The authors would specifically like to thank Amarnatha Reddy, Pritam, Meenal Gupta, Satya Thopalli, TV Sharma, Ram Kiran Kanumuri, CV Sreekanth, Ravi Ganti, Chanakya Sehgal, Deepa, and others who wanted to remain anonymous for their inputs that have been incorporated in the study. A huge thank you to Mr. Pravin Thangavelu of RSP Science Hub, the editor of the International Research Journal on Advanced Science Hub (https://rspsciencehub.com/), who has always supported the authors in their research and publications. A heartfelt thank you to the book editors for giving us an opportunity to publish the chapter in their professionally crafted book.

REFERENCES

Banerjee, P., Pandey, J., Gupta, M. (2019). Practical Applications of HR Analytics, a step-by-step guide. *Sage Publishing*, New Delhi. ISBN: 9789353282967.

Bersin, J. Bersin, Josh (Host). (2023, June 10) The Changing Role of Data and People Analytics in HR. [Audio Podcast Episode]. Josh Bersin. Available from: https://joshbersin.com/podcast/the-changing-role-of-data-and-people-analytics-in-hr/.

Chakraborty, P. (2023, August, 27) Personal Communication. [WhatsApp]..

Collier, D., Schallenback, C.L. (2017) HR Shared Services (HRSS): Model and Trends, Fall 2017 – CAHRS RA Project, White Paper. Retrieved from : https://ecommons.cornell.edu/handle/1813/73716.

Coy, C. (2017, February 17) On the Four Stages of Workforce Analytics. Where Are you? Retrieved from: https://www.tlnt.com/articles/four-stages-of-workforce-analytics.

Deepa (2023) Personal Communication. [WhatsApp]..

Van den Heuvel, S., Bondarouk, T. (2016) The Rise (and Fall) of HR Analytics, a study into the future applications, value, structure, and system support. Retrieved from: https://ris.utwenten.nl/ws/portalfiles/portal/13277560/Van+den+Heuvel+Bondarouk+2016+HRIC+Sidney+-+Metis.pdf.

IBM (n.d.) Strategic Workforce Planning. Retrieved from: https://www.ibm.com/products/planning-analytics/workforce-planning?utm_content=SRCWW&p1=Search&p4=43700076548887592&p5=p&gclid=CjwKCAjwxaanBhBQEiwA84TVXOVLGCMhhI8Qfd1KIYvakJo6Tw8BRBhYueWTrTe_oS23IOh1lGhnzRoCMpgQAvD_BwE&gclsrc=aw.ds.

Infosys (n.d.A) Infosys People Analytics and insights, overview. Retrieved from: https://www.infosys.com/services/oracle/offerings/people-analytics-insights.html.

Infosys (n.d.B) Grow your talent with enhanced visibility into performance, overview. Retrieved from: https://www.infosys.com/industries/professional-services/offerings/human-capital-management.html.

Infotechlead (2023, April 24) Aramco selects Infosys to brings insights to HR data and analytics. Retrieved from: https://infotechlead.com/software/aramco-selectxs-infosys-to-bring-insights-to-hr-data-and-analytics-78019.

Kanumuri, R.K. (2023, June 2) Personal Communication [Telephonic Discussion].

Komm, A., Pollner, F., Schaninger, B., Sikka, S. (2021, March 12) The new possible: How HR can help build the organization of the future. Retrieved from: https://www.mckinsey.com/capabailities/people-an--organizational-performance/our-insights/the-new-possible-how-hr-can-help-build-the-organzation-of-the-future.

Marler, H., Janet & Boudreau, W., John (2016) An evidence-based review of HR Analytics. International Journal of Human Resource Management, 28(1), 3–26. [http://dx.doi.org/10.1080/09585192.2016.1244699]

NASSCOM (2023) Priming for No Normal future, Technology Sector in India, Strategic Review 2023. Retrieved from: https://nasscom.in/knowledge-center/publications/technology-sector- india-2023-strateg-c-review#:~:text=In%20FY2023%2C%20India%27s%20technology%20industry,11.4%25%20in%20constant%20currency%20terms.

Network Perspective (n.d.) Ethics in People Analytics. Retrieved from: https://www. networkperspective.io/ethics-in-people-analytics#:~:text=What%20is%20People%20Analytics%3F,analyzing%2C%20and%20reporting%20HR%20data.

Oracle (2021) The State of HR Analytics 2021. HR Research Institute. Retrieved from: https://www.oracle.com/a/ocom/docs/application/human-capital-management/h-t-talent-analytics-hrdotcom.pdf.

People Data Labs (2022, February 17) How Advanced HR analytics enhances your HR Operations. Retrieved from: https://blog.peopledatalabs.com/post/how-advanced-hr-analytics-enhances-your-hr-operations.

Reddy, A. (2023, July 4). Personal Communication. [Discussion]..

Reddy, P., Raghunadha & Lakshmikeethi, P., (2017) HR Analytics-An effective evidence based HRM tool. International Journal of Business and Management Invention, 6(7), 23-34. Retrieved from: https://www.semanticscholar.org/paper/'-Hr-Analytics-'-An-Effective-Evidence-Based-HRM-Reddy-Lakshmikeerthi/0af8cfea65ce09150a92af8a8800b8ab32febac5.

Roy, S. (2020, October 19) TCS launches HR-tech analytics tool for talent management. Retrieved from: https://www.techcircle.in/2020/10/19/tcs-launches-hr-tech-analytics-tool-for-talent-management.

Scanlon, A., Scott (2021) How HR can help build the organizations of the future. Retrieved from: https://huntscalnon.com/how-hr-can-help-build-the-organization-of-the-future.

Sehgal, C. (2023, April 2) Personal Communication [Telephonic Communication].

Sharma, T.V. (2023, July 23) Personal Communication [Discussion].

Singh, D. (2023, June 22) Role of Analytics and Data in Human Resource Management. Retrieved from: https://www.linkedin.com/pulse/role-analytics-data-human-resource-management-deependra-singh/.

Sreekanth, C.V. (2022, December 7) Personal Communication [Telephonic Communication].

Sun, S. (2022, August 17) IT-BPM Industry employment in India FY 2009-2022. Statista. Retrieved from: https://www.statista.com/statistics/320729/india-it-industry-direct-indirect-employment/#:~:text=The%20Indian% 20information%20technology%20and,IT%2companies%20across%20 the%20globe.

TCS (2020, October 19) TCS' New Workforce Analytics solution to help companies attract and retain the right digital talent. TCS Press Release. Retrieved from: https://www.tcs.com/who-we-are/newsroom/press-release/tcs-new-workforce-analytics-solution-to-help-companies-attract-and-retain-the-right-digital-talent.

Thopalli, S. (2023, April 4) Personal Communication [Telephonic Communication].

U-next (2020, November 11) State of People Analytics and Digital HR in India in 2020. Retrieved from: https://unext.com/blogs/hr-analytics/state-of-people-analytics-digital-hr-in-india-in-2020/.

Ulrich, Dave (1997) Human resource champions: The next agenda for adding value and delivering results. Boston: Harvard Business School Press. ISBN: 9780875847191.

Vulpen, Erik van (n.d.) What is HR Analytics? All you need to know to get started. Retrieved from: https://www.aihr.com/blog/what-is-hr-analytics/.

World, H.R. (2020, October 20) TCS launches workforce analytics solution. Economic Times HR World. Retrieved from: https://hr.economictimes.indiatimes.com/news/hrtech/tcs/-launches-workforce-analytcs-solutions/78761325.

CHAPTER 2

Impact of HR Analytics on Organizational Performance: A Modern Approach in HR

Nidhi Srivastava[1,*] and **Isha Bhardwaj**[1,*]

[1] *IMS - Ghaziabad (University Courses Campus), Dehli, India*

Abstract: The field of human resource analytics, characterized by its emphasis on data-driven and analytical approaches within human resources management, is rapidly emerging as a critical element in organizational contexts. Our work environments are evolving due to the swift integration of data and information processing advancements with the progress of human resources management (HRM). This paper explores the existing body of research on HR analytics and its significance in making predictive decisions within organizations. HRM is centered on identifying tools and metrics, founded on the fundamental principle that employers and employees can collaborate to achieve shared objectives within the hierarchical structure of an organization. In such a dynamic landscape, human resources remain a pivotal distinguishing factor for any organization, presenting opportunities for competitive growth and the creation of essential organizational value.

Keywords: Decision-making, HR analytics, Predictive.

INTRODUCTION

Human resource management focuses on optimizing the utilization of personnel to achieve both organizational and individual objectives. This encompasses tasks such as recruitment, administration, and exit procedures within the organization. A crucial facet of HR involves assessing employee performance and designing training initiatives to enhance their skills. The emergence of HR as a distinct field was accompanied by a specific focus on performance management. This practice involves continuous interaction between managers and employees to attain organizational targets while fostering individual growth.

Performance management entails a dynamic exchange of expectations, goal setting, ongoing feedback, and performance evaluation. It establishes a channel of

* **Corresponding authors Nidhi Srivastava and Isha Bhardwaj:** IMS - Ghaziabad (University Courses Campus), Dehli, India; E-mails: nidhi.mzpshanker@gmail.com, ishabhardwaj@imsuc.ac.in

communication that develops throughout the year, aiming to fulfill both organizational and personal aims. Managers analyze gathered data to comprehend employee performance and bridge any gaps identified in the data. Tools like HR analytics are employed to accumulate this data. HR analytics involves collecting and leveraging talent-related data to enhance crucial workforce aspects. This data-driven approach aids in decision-making, foreseeing employee turnover, recognizing high-performers, and identifying skill enhancement needs. Also termed people analytics, HR analytics empowers organizations to gauge the influence of HR metrics on overall business outcomes, facilitating informed decisions guided by data.

Four types of HR analytics are explained below (Fig. **1**):

- Descriptive Analytics
- Diagnostic Analytics
- Predictive Analytics
- Prescriptive Analytics

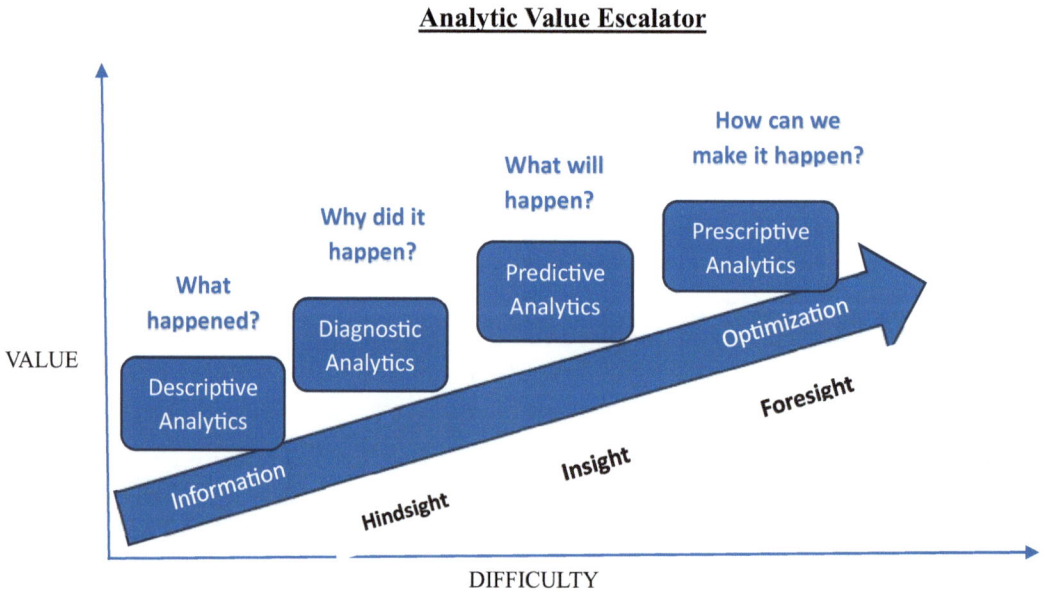

Fig. (1). Types of HR analytics.

© 2022 IJRAR August 2022, Volume 9, Issue 3 www.ijrar.org (E-ISSN 2348-12earl). Performance Management is an important aspect in Human Resources as it is a continuous communication process between managers and employees to achieve organizational goals as well as develop personnel skills of employees. This entire communication process involves defining clear specific expectations, establishing goals, providing continuous feedback and examining results. Performance Management builds a communication system between a manager and employee that is built throughout the year in hope of accomplishing organizational as well as individual goals. To understand employee managers, go through all the collected data and addresses the performance gaps through the given data. Various tools are used to gather such data like HR Analytics. HR Analytic is the collection and application of talent data to improve critical talent. It is basically used for decision making using the available data, to predict employee turnover and identify better performers or predict skills that need to be Improved. HR Analytics is also known as people analytics. It enables your organization to measure the impact of HR metrics on overall business performances and make decision based on the data.

Descriptive Analytics

Gathering raw data doesn't make sense and isn't always useful, but once it is sorted and put in a Descriptive analysis (often referred to as observation and reporting) represents the foundational level of analysis and is commonly employed. Its primary function is to compile all accessible historical data and condense it into a comprehensible format. For instance, tallying the number of employees within the organization or a specific department falls within the purview of descriptive analytics. Similarly, more intricate measurements, such as turnover, are also encompassed within descriptive analytics. This form of analysis involves scrutinizing historical data with the goal of elucidating past occurrences.

Diagnostic Analytics

While descriptive analytics reveals occurrences, diagnostic analytics uncovers the reasons behind them. It surpasses the understanding of the "what" and delves into the quest for the "why" behind these events. This process entails making observations, acknowledging the findings from descriptive analysis, and then advancing into conducting diagnostic analysis. Diagnostic analytics employs a range of methodologies, encompassing techniques like data drilling and data mining. These approaches are utilized to delve into the fundamental triggers of issues and unearth potential remedies. In order to fathom the origins of problems and devise solutions, it is essential for companies to comprehend the underlying causes driving these issues.

Predictive Analytics

Descriptive analytics is rooted in historical data, essentially looking back in time. On the other hand, predictive analytics takes a forward-looking stance, employing diverse statistical models and projections to anticipate future scenarios. The primary objective of this analysis is to identify the organization's requirements. These models are constructed based on patterns identified through descriptive analytics. They can aid in foreseeing factors such as an employee's tenure within the organization or assist the talent acquisition department in evaluating an employee's alignment with the company's culture.

Prescriptive Analytics

Once future scenarios have been predicted, the subsequent question revolves around actionable steps. This is where prescriptive analytics comes into play, offering recommendations based on both forecasts and historical data. This form of analysis proves particularly valuable for businesses dealing with fluctuating demand, such as seasonal patterns. For instance, a retail company might seek insights into optimal holiday staffing levels. Moreover, prescriptive analytics can extend to decisions like hiring new personnel and factoring in their skills and competencies across their entire employment journey. Essentially, this approach leverages available information at various stages to prescribe the most suitable actions. The data itself becomes the guide for future steps. Contemporary organizations rely on a range of professional HR analytical tools, including but not limited to Visier, Tableau, QLIK, SPSS, and Microsoft Excel.

Human Resource Analytics (HR Analytics)

The utilization of HR analytics tools proves highly advantageous for organizations in assessing their strengths and areas that need improvement. The outcomes of this HR research should illustrate the advantages a company gains from dedicating resources to its human capital. In contemporary discussions, terms like people analytics and workforce analytics are occasionally used interchangeably with HR Analytics. It is essential to grasp how analytics can drive HR forward in this context (Opatha, 2020).

The employee journey is shaped by a range of interactions that occur over the course of their employment cycle. Each day an employee experiences a stride along their path, during which they observe their surroundings and engage with colleagues and systems, yielding valuable insights (Gaur, 2020). Utilizing HR analytics, you can systematically collect data at every phase, enabling the formulation of strategies to enrich the work environment. This might involve refining existing processes or devising novel ones. When employees see their input being considered in decision-making, they feel valued. Cultivating this trust among your workforce has the potential to amplify both retention rates and overall engagement levels (Bapna *et al.*, 2013).

Benefits of HR Analytics

• Utilizing predictive analytics in HR helps identify problematic practices that contribute to employee attrition, ultimately aiding in the retention of high-performing staff.

• It allows for the transparent presentation of results and the methods used to achieve them.

• HR analytics plays a crucial role in human resource planning by assisting in forecasting employee needs and the necessary skill sets to meet organizational goals. It also facilitates unbiased sourcing of top talent for specific positions.

• Improved performance outcomes in organizations are attainable through well-informed decision-making, particularly in the realm of talent acquisition.

• It assists in identifying critical performance areas that can have a significant impact on overall organizational performance.

• HR analytics tools often feature data visualization and automation, which can automatically pinpoint areas of weakness, outline team skill requirements, and design programs to address those needs.

Organizational Performance Metrics

Organizations employ three primary approaches to assess their performance, namely productivity, effectiveness, and industry ranking. Esteemed management authority Peter F. Drucker emphasized the need for personnel to comprehend the connection between their actions and outcomes, underscoring the significance of performance (Gurusinghe *et al.*, 2021). According to Drucker's assertion that "Performance must be the organization's principal focus and the organization's driving principle:, managers should predefine performance indicators to enable employees to correlate actions with high-performance goals (Arora *et al.*, 2022). The central metrics frequently adopted for evaluating organizational performance encompass productivity, effectiveness, and industry rankings (Shyaa, 2019).

Productivity

Productivity is gauged by dividing the total output of goods or services by the inputs required to generate that output. Organizations dedicate substantial efforts to achieve favorable outcomes, aiming to maximize outputs with minimal input expenditure (Pillai & Sivathanu, 2021a). The organization's productivity is quantified by sales revenue from goods and services (selling price multiplied by the quantity sold). Input evaluation involves assessing costs linked to acquiring and converting organizational resources into outputs (Mondore & Carson, 2011). Enhancing productivity necessitates optimizing output prices while curtailing input costs, essentially refining the execution of organizational tasks. Thus, organizational productivity serves as an indicator of employees' proficiency in task execution (Pillai & Sivathanu, 2021b).

Organizational Effectiveness

Organizational effectiveness pertains to the extent to which a company attains its goals in a pragmatic manner. This widely used performance metric aligns with diverse definitions proposed by management researchers. The effectiveness of an organization is founded on its adeptness in leveraging available resources and adapting to its environment. Though these models help assess specific facets of organizational performance, the ultimate focus remains on how well objectives are met (Ali *et al.*, 2019). Managers rely on this information to shape strategies, processes, job roles, and employee efforts (Otoo, 2019).

Industry Ranking

Naisa *et al.*, 2020 concluded that Industries are ranked based on key performance indicators. Notably, Fortune 500 companies' performance is ranked using financial metrics such as profitability, return on sales, and return on equity). Industry Week's best-managed firms, including attributes like financial performance, innovation, leadership, globalization, partnerships, employee development, and community involvement, use metrics such as growth in revenue per employee, revenue per unit of assets, and earnings growth over different timeframes (Durai *et al.*, 2022). Given the diversity in evaluation criteria, different agencies apply distinct metrics to assess organizational effectiveness within specific sectors or industries (Kadiresan *et al.*, 2015)

HR analytics can gauge various productivity metrics, such as absenteeism rates and revenue generated per employee. Elevated absenteeism not only escalates staffing costs but also reduces overall productivity, potentially reflecting employee well-being and morale (Naisa *et al.*, 2020). The computation of revenue per employee involves dividing the total income by the number of full-time equivalent (FTE) employees. This metric indicates the average revenue contribution made by each employee to the organization's financial performance (Pillai & Sivathanu, 2021). However, to present a comprehensive view of the company's profitability, labor expenses should also be factored in (Manoharan *et al.*, 2022).

Proposed Conceptual Model

The authors constructed a conceptual model (Fig. **2**. Conceptual Model) that integrates insights from both scholarly literature and recommendations from practitioners within the domains of human capital management, HR analytics, and organizational performance. They proceeded to formulate the following hypotheses:

Hypothesis (1a)

The constituent elements of human capital management exert a substantial impact on organizational performance.

Hypothesis (1b)

The presence of HR analytics acts as a mediating factor between human capital management and organizational performance.

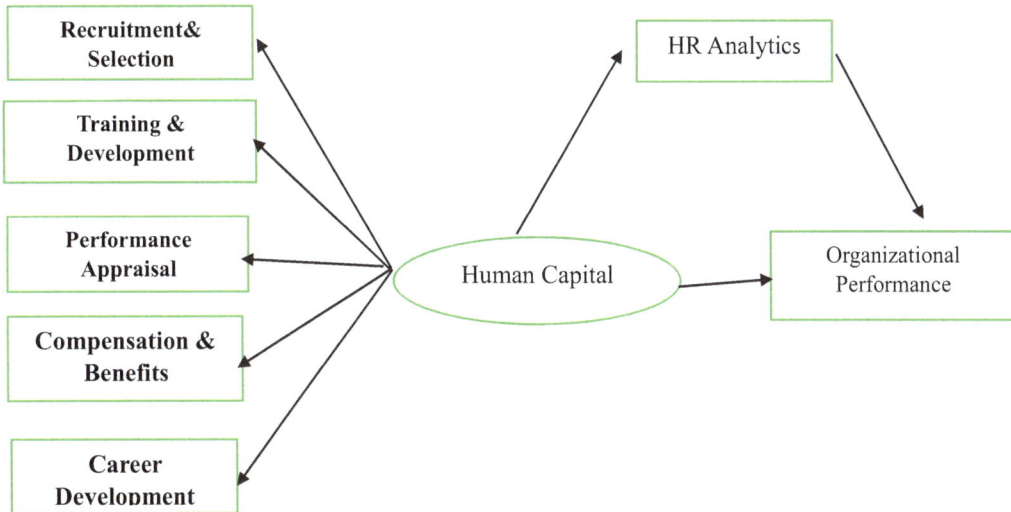

Fig. (2). Author conceptual model.

Objectives of the Study

• This research aims to assess how the integration of HR analytics influences organizational performance within the context of human capital management.

• To investigate the influence of different aspects of human capital management on organizational performance while considering the mediating role of HR analytics.

METHODOLOGY

The research is grounded in an extensive review of relevant literature, encompassing both published and unpublished sources. The investigation involves an analysis of references, authors, subjects, citations, and journals from various studies, as well as insights from practitioners. The primary objective of this endeavor is to explore the influence of human capital management (HCM) on organizational performance, with a specific focus on the intermediary role played by HR analytics in connecting HCM with organizational performance. The study is designed to formulate a comprehensive research framework.

Secondary Data Analysis

Here are some examples of companies using HR analytics for organizational development:

Google

Google is a pioneer in the use of HR analytics, and they have used it to completely reinvent HR within their organization. They use a data-driven approach to everything from recruitment to performance management, and they have been able to achieve significant results. For example, Google has used HR analytics to identify the most effective ways to recruit top talent, and they have also used it to develop programs to improve employee engagement and retention.

Use of HR Analytics at Google

By using HR analytics, Google developed a program called "Project Oxygen," which combines employee feedback and productivity data to analyze employee behavior and skills. This program identifies what successful managers do. From this data, Google was able to determine 10 key behaviors of great managers.

Result for HR Analytics (Google)

The project helped train future business leaders and enhanced the performance of management teams. Employees emphasized soft skills and emotional intelligence over hard technical skills.

Microsoft

Microsoft has also been a leader in the use of HR analytics, and they have used it to improve a variety of HR processes. For example, Microsoft has used HR analytics to develop statistical profiles of employees who are more likely to leave the company. This information has allowed Microsoft to target these employees with retention programs, which has helped to reduce turnover.

Use of HR Analytics (Microsoft)

Microsoft leverages HR analytics to enhance its workforce management and drive organizational success. By analyzing employee data, Microsoft identifies trends and patterns related to performance, retention, and engagement. This data-driven approach helps the company tailor programs and initiatives to meet the specific needs of its employees. For instance, Microsoft uses HR analytics to design effective training programs, optimize talent acquisition processes, and develop strategies to boost employee satisfaction and productivity. Through HR analytics, Microsoft can make informed decisions that foster a supportive and dynamic work environment, ultimately contributing to the company's overall competitiveness and innovation.

Results of HR Analytics at Microsoft

Microsoft's HR analytics initiatives have significantly improved the training of future business leaders and enhanced the performance of management teams. Through the analysis of employee data, Microsoft identified the importance of focusing on soft skills and emotional intelligence over hard technical skills. This shift has led to more effective leadership development and a more cohesive and productive management team.

HP

Hewlett-Packard (HP) used HR analytics to tackle high employee turnover in their sales division. They analyzed data such as performance reviews, compensation, and tenure to identify employees who were at risk of leaving. This information allowed HP to develop targeted interventions to keep these employees, such as providing them with additional training or opportunities for advancement.

Use of HR Analytics at HP

HP employs HR analytics to optimize its workforce management and drive organizational success. By systematically analyzing employee data, HP identifies critical trends related to performance, engagement, and retention. This data-driven approach allows HP to design tailored training programs, improve talent acquisition processes, and develop strategies that enhance employee satisfaction and productivity. HR analytics at HP has also emphasized the importance of soft skills and emotional intelligence, leading to more effective leadership development and a stronger, more cohesive management team. Overall, HR analytics enables HP to make informed decisions that foster innovation and competitiveness within the company.

Results of HR Analytics at HP

HP's use of HR analytics has led to improved leadership development and enhanced management team performance by focusing on soft skills and emotional intelligence. This data-driven approach has also increased employee satisfaction and productivity.

IBM

IBM used HR analytics to reduce turnover for critical roles. They used a machine learning algorithm that included data from sources such as recruitment, performance, and employee sentiment. This algorithm helped IBM to identify employees who were at risk of leaving, and they were able to take steps to retain these employees.

Use of HR Analytics at IBM

At IBM, HR analytics plays a crucial role in optimizing talent management strategies. By analyzing employee data, IBM identifies trends related to performance, engagement, and retention, enabling the company to tailor programs and initiatives to meet the specific needs of its workforce. This data-driven approach enhances talent acquisition processes, improves employee development programs, and fosters a culture of continuous improvement and innovation throughout the organization.

Results of HR Analytics at IBM

The results of HR analytics at IBM include improved talent management strategies, enhanced employee engagement, and increased retention rates. By leveraging data insights, IBM has optimized talent acquisition processes, identified areas for skill development, and fostered a culture of innovation and continuous improvement. Overall, HR analytics at IBM has contributed to a more productive and satisfied workforce, driving the company's success in the dynamic business landscape.

Unilever

Unilever used HR analytics to manage a crisis situation. When Kraft Heinz launched a hostile takeover bid, Unilever's workforce analytics team analyzed employee networks and sentiment to track how employees were reacting to the situation. This information helped Unilever to develop effective defense strategies.

Use of HR Analytics at Unilever

At Unilever, HR analytics is utilized to drive strategic workforce decisions and improve organizational effectiveness. By analyzing employee data, Unilever identifies trends related to performance, engagement, and retention, enabling the company to make informed decisions about talent acquisition, development, and retention strategies. HR analytics at Unilever also supports diversity and inclusion initiatives by providing insights into workforce demographics and trends. Overall, HR analytics plays a critical role in Unilever's talent management practices, helping the company to maintain a competitive edge in the market and achieve its business objectives.

Results of HR Analytics at Unilever

The results of HR analytics at Unilever encompass improved talent management strategies, enhanced employee engagement, and increased retention rates. By leveraging data insights, Unilever has optimized its recruitment processes, identified skill gaps, and developed targeted training programs to support employee development. Additionally, HR analytics has enabled Unilever to enhance diversity and inclusion initiatives by providing valuable insights into workforce demographics and trends. Overall, the implementation of HR analytics at Unilever has led to more informed decision-making and a more effective and engaged workforce, driving the company's success in the competitive market landscape.

Literature Review

Two key responsibilities of human capital management (HCM) involve the processes of recruitment and selection. These steps encompass job analysis and workforce planning, which collectively shape a company's performance (W, 2016). Often, a corporation's most valuable asset is considered to be its human resources. The introduction to this essay delves into the recruitment and selection process. As indicated by Ben-Gal *et al.* in 2022, additional metrics to consider in the hiring process encompass factors like "fill time", measured by calculating the duration between creating a job requisition and filling it. The selection and recruitment should prioritize choosing the best-suited individuals, devising career plans for employees, providing training and mentorship, fostering a culture of high performance, and closely monitoring employee performance (Arora *et al.*, 2021). To maximize the potential of its workforce, a company must possess a deep understanding of its employees. Executing human capital strategies necessitates well-defined procedures and actions for project success, including the availability of reliable resources, a budget, and established deadlines, all of which are outlined by Ferreira *et al.* in 2022. In a similar vein, R. Karthik (2012) concluded that training objectives elucidate the learner's expectations subsequent to completing a training course.

According to Davis and Bates (2010), a training program's effectiveness hinges on the trainee's ability to apply the theoretical concepts acquired during the training in their actual workplace. They emphasized the importance of using methods such as role-playing, case studies, simulations, mediated exercises, and computer-based learning to ensure that employees possess current and relevant knowledge and can apply it to real-world situations.

R. Karthik (2012) further highlighted that training objectives serve as a means to clarify the learner's expectations following the completion of a training course. These objectives are crucial from the perspectives of the trainer, trainee, designer, and evaluator. As noted by Ahmad and Shahzad (2011), employee performance within an organization is influenced by various factors, including compensation practices, performance evaluation procedures, and promotion processes.

Naisa *et al.* (2020) concluded that within organizations, the assessment and measurement of various sub-departments related to human resources, such as recruitment, selection, training, compensation, motivation, performance appraisal, employee well-being, and grievance management, are conducted using performance metrics. These metrics are used to establish a connection between information-gathering and decision-making processes. This research primarily focuses on examining the impact of performance evaluations on individual outcomes, organizational results, productivity, and overall performance (Palshikar *et al.*, 2017). The study asserts that the concept and implementation of employee compensation revolve around the principles of internal fairness and external competitiveness, as highlighted by (Ben-Gal *et al.* in 2022).

Thomas and Tymon (2009) conducted an assessment that identified four intrinsic motivation elements related to career development: meaningfulness, development, choice, and competence.

In some industries, achieving career success is heavily influenced by luck, and it is important to acknowledge that career planning alone does not guarantee success. As per research conducted by Dalia Rosa *et al.* (2020), Kang & Kaur (2020), Park *et al.* (2020), Verma & Kesari (2020), Wong *et al.* (2020), and Zuo *et al.* (2020), it is emphasized that employees should actively engage in professional planning to remain prepared for potential career opportunities. Successful businesses often implement career planning as a strategic tool to align with their objectives. Given that human capital management (HCM) places significant emphasis on fostering individual employee growth while incorporating various functional aspects of HR management, this study primarily focuses on career development (Saleem & Amin, 2013).

HR analytics addresses challenges related to employee engagement and productivity. Kale *et al.* (2022) explored how HR analytics can transform HR from a transactional role to a strategic one. By leveraging data, HR can improve core functions like recruitment, talent management, and employee engagement, ultimately leading to increased productivity and reduced turnover.

Davenport *et al.* (2010) further emphasized the global relevance of HR analytics, arguing that it strengthens the strategic value of HR by enabling evidence-based decision-making. This aligns with research by Malik and Allam (2021), who demonstrated how organizations like Google utilize HR analytics to refine their recruitment processes and identify top talent.

The international literature provides compelling evidence of how HR analytics can positively influence various organizational performance indicators. ResearchGate publications explore the connection between HR analytics and improved quality of hire, reduced absenteeism, and increased employee satisfaction (Hritik Kale *et al.*, 2022).

Global Perspectives on HR Analytics

North America

Companies in North America, particularly in the United States, are at the forefront of integrating HR analytics into their operations. A study by Deloitte (2020) found that 70% of large organizations in the US utilize some form of HR analytics, primarily for talent acquisition and performance management.

Europe

European firms are increasingly adopting HR analytics to comply with stringent labor regulations and enhance workforce diversity. The Chartered Institute of Personnel and Development (CIPD) reports that over 60% of UK companies are investing in HR analytics to improve employee retention and satisfaction.

Asia-Pacific

In the Asia-Pacific region, HR analytics adoption is growing rapidly, driven by the need to manage large, diverse workforces. A report by PwC (2021) indicates that organizations in countries like India, China, and Australia are using HR analytics.

Organizational Performance

Daft (2000) asserted that organizational performance is the resultant outcome, contrasting with the intended development that organizations envision. Kiran, Shanmugam, Raju, and Kanagasabapathy (2022) emphasized in their study the impact of human capital management on organizational performance with the mediating effect of human resource analytics. Recardo (2001) differentiated performance from productivity, indicating that performance encompasses attributes such as value, consistency, proficiency, and worth, while productivity focuses solely on effort expended within a specific timeframe.

Appraisals of organizational performance significantly impact its reputation. In high-performing companies, managers adeptly oversee resources to maximize value. This entails activities encompassing asset acquisition, maintenance, replacement, and divestment, constituting asset management (Sivathanu & Pillai, 2020). Asset management is a concern across all managerial levels, as decisions rely on resource optimization, be it personnel, data, equipment, and more (Sivathanu & Pillai, 2019). Strategies for effective asset management are vital for sustained organizational performance, as managers strive to excel in key performance indicators assessed internally and externally (Mishra *et al.*, 2018). Delivering value to customers is pivotal for businesses, and monitoring value provision is achieved through performance assessment (Khayinga & Muathe, 2018).

An organization tends to experience benefits and financial gains when it enjoys a strong reputation and is in good financial standing. Research on the correlation between reputation and financial success, conducted by McCartney and Fu in 2021, found that positive goodwill is closely associated with positive economic indicators such as returns and profit growth. Understanding the connection between information and action is best achieved through practical knowledge. Within an organization, individuals should actively share their experiences and apply them to improve work processes, methodologies, or products, all with the aim of enhancing overall organizational performance (Otoo, 2019).

Assessing performance serves as a critical aspect of monitoring an organization's progress, involving the comparison of achieved results or outcomes with the organization's intended objectives. However, the process of performance measurement typically adopts a top-down approach for defining performance criteria, which differs from the bottom-up approach commonly found in many organizations. In most cases, specific departments are responsible for determining what aspects to measure, such as the average weekly working hours of employees, while other departments may prioritize evaluating employees' performance and the quality of their work as more crucial factors (Manoharan *et al.*, 2022). Performance outcomes refer to the comprehensive evaluation of work that directly impacts the organization and aligns with both organizational and departmental strategic goals, playing a vital role in the business process (Ferreira *et al.*, 2022). To establish criteria for identifying essential business processes, it is essential to consider assessing the effectiveness of the work performed (Nain *et al.*, 2022).

The Influence of HR Analytics as a Mediator of Organizational Performance within The Context of Human Capital Management

Kamran Asif *et al.* (2015) emphasized that HR fulfills the fundamental needs of internal departments. Recruitment entails identifying potential candidates for current or future roles within the organization. Engaging with current or potential job seekers is an integral aspect of the recruitment process. Given the fierce competition in today's business landscape, organizations can no longer rely solely on their products or services to gain a competitive edge. Chaturvedi (2016) proposed that HR analytics goes beyond merely adopting successful HR practices from other organizations; it can set an organization apart from its competitors and provide a distinct competitive advantage. Spahic (2015) illustrated that HR analytics has the capacity to predict employee or customer attrition to competitors, forecast the potential consequences of critical organizational decisions, and optimize consumer offerings, thereby enhancing competitiveness. Naula (2015) further highlighted that effective and strategic decisions not only enhance an organization's credibility but also establish HR as a core function. To substantiate this claim, researchers ought to conduct ROI-based surveys, analyze cost-saving benefits, and promote efficient practices. As businesses increasingly embrace big data, new perspectives facilitated by sentiment analysis, network analysis, and machine learning are greatly benefiting workforce and enterprise management.

According to Opatha (2020), performing HR analytics demands a distinct skill set compared to conventional HR practitioners. Given that HR analytics emerges from the intersection of business and technology, there could be notable advantages for organizations to establish a dedicated team or unit specifically focused on HR analytics. The widespread adoption of HR Analytics is fundamentally reshaping the landscape of HR. Consequently, organizations should prioritize their HR departments, enabling them to assume a more strategic role in achieving corporate objectives and goals (Dahlbom *et al.*, 2020). HR professionals must reevaluate existing HR policies and procedures to effectively implement HR analytics in each functional area. They should offer guidance to departments on leveraging technology and analytics tools to maximize their benefits (Marler & Boudreau, 2017). The timing of evaluating the value of workforce analytics in relation to HRA and organizational performance has also been emphasized by Opatha (2020).

Implications of the Study

The research paper offers insights for scholars and professionals in the field of human capital management, focusing on how incorporating advanced HR analytics tools can boost overall organizational performance. The paper also outlines recommendations for future researchers to practically test the suggested theoretical framework and formulate hypotheses across various types of organizations. The research presents empirical proof that the utilization of HR analytics can effectively enhance business performance by streamlining the management of human capital. Furthermore, the study offers a significant contribution to companies aiming to enhance their HR technological capacities or extend their existing HR analytics initiatives.

DISCUSSION AND CONCLUSION

The organization needs to address questions like "Why should employees stay with our company?" HR analytics allows you to calculate what employees need or are lacking and then create a system or a program that will help increase performance and retention rates. Companies like Google use HR analytics to collect employee performance data to determine the most effective training programs to help both high and low-performing employees. HR analytics and other unrecognized organizational methods that are related to HR analytics are ignored by many organizations. The study focuses on how HR practices can be used to change traditional roles to transformational roles in organizations. The study tries to explore and understand the role of analytics in this modern era. The increase in expectations in performance has put the focus on HR analytics to create a new innovative and competitive world at work. To execute the role effectively, HR managers and leaders need considerable support from their organizational leaders. First, they need to be able to go in depth of the problem. These problems can come from various issues, and experts in areas such as a change in management, leadership development, staffing and metrics, and HR analytics can help analyze the situation and provide possible solutions for these problems.

According to Moliterno and Ployhart's 2011 study, utilizing their model, a higher level of organizational human capital management is a direct outcome of a higher level of individual human capital management. They also observed a positive and direct connection between HCM and "aggregated individual human capital". Ployhart's framework is introduced as a valuable tool for managing human capital. The study further elucidates how the integration of HR analytics into human capital management has a significant impact on an organization's overall operational effectiveness.

REFERENCES

Alabi, E.Z.E.K.I.E.L., Afolabi, M. A., & Adeyemo, S. A. (2015). Influence of E-recruitment on Organizational Performance in Nigeria. In The Academic Conference of African Scholar Publications & Research International on Achieving Unprecedented Transformation in a fastmoving World: Agenda for Sub-Sahara Africa (Vol. 3, No. 3).

Ali, Z., Bashir, M., Mehreen, A. (2019). Managing organizational effectiveness through talent management and career development: The mediating role of employee engagement. *Journal of Management Sciences, 6*(1), 62-78.
[http://dx.doi.org/10.20547/jms.2014.1906105]

Angrave, D., Charlwood, A., Kirkpatrick, I., Lawrence, M., Stuart, M. (2016). HR and analytics: why HR is set to fail the big data challenge. *Hum. Resour. Manage. J., 26*(1), 1-11.
[http://dx.doi.org/10.1111/1748-8583.12090]

Anwar, G., Abdullah, N.N. (2021). The impact of Human resource management practice on Organizational performance. *Int. J. Eng. Bus. Manag., 5.*

Angrave, D., Charlwood, A., Kirkpatrick, I., Lawrence, M., Stuart, M. (2016). HR and analytics: why HR is set to fail the big data challenge. *Hum. Resour. Manage. J., 26*(1), 1-11.
[http://dx.doi.org/10.1111/1748-8583.12090]

Chalutz Ben-Gal, H. (2019). An ROI-based review of HR analytics: practical implementation tools. *Person. Rev., 48*(6), 1429-1448.
[http://dx.doi.org/10.1108/PR-11-2017-0362]

Cayrat, C., Boxall, P. (2022). Exploring the phenomenon of HR analytics: a study of challenges, risks and impacts in 40 large companics. *Journal of Organizational Effectiveness: People and Performance, 9*(4), 572-590.
[http://dx.doi.org/10.1108/JOEPP-08-2021-0238]

Fitz-Enz, J. (2010). *The new HR analytics.* American Management Association.

Henriksen, K. G., & Johansson, S. H. H. (2021). HR analytics and Organizational Performance (Master's thesis, Handelshøyskolen BI).

Kiran, V. S., Shanmugam, V., Raju, R. K., & Kanagasabapathy, J. R. (2022). Impact of human capital management on organizational performance with the mediation effect of human resource analytics.

International journal of professional business review, 7(3), e0667-e0667. Beardwell, J., & Claydon, T. (Eds.). (2007). *Human resource management: A contemporary approach.* Pearson Education. [http://dx.doi.org/10.26668/businessreview/2022.v7i3.0667]

Kale, H., Aher, D., Anute, N. (2022). HR Analytics and its Impact on Organizations Performance. *International Journal of Research and Analytical Reviews,* 9(3), 619-630.

Levenson, A. (2015). *Strategic analytics: Advancing strategy execution and organizational effectiveness.* Berrett-Koehler Publishers.

Qamar, Y., Samad, T.A. (2022). Human resource analytics: a review and bibliometric analysis. *Person. Rev., 51*(1), 251-283.
[http://dx.doi.org/10.1108/PR-04-2020-0247]

Thakral, P., Srivastava, P.R., Dash, S.S., Jasimuddin, S.M., Zhang, Z.J. (2023). Trends in the thematic landscape of HR analytics research: a structural topic modeling approach. *Manage. Decis., 61*(12), 3665-3690.
[http://dx.doi.org/10.1108/MD-01-2023-0080]

Margherita, A. (2022). Human resources analytics: A systematization of research topics and directions for future research. *Hum. Resour. Manage. Rev., 32*(2), 100795.
[http://dx.doi.org/10.1016/j.hrmr.2020.100795]

Muhammad, S., Khan, I., Hameed, F. (2021). The Impact of Performance Management System on Employees Performance. *International Journal of Business and Management Sciences,* 2(3), 38-47.

Reddy, P.R., Lakshmikeerthi, P. (2017). HR analytics–an effective evidence based HRM tool. *International Journal of Business and Management Invention,* 6(7), 23-34.

Sharma, A., Sharma, T. (2017). HR analytics and performance appraisal system. *Manag. Res. Rev., 40*(6), 684-697.
[http://dx.doi.org/10.1108/MRR-04-2016-0084]

Opatha, H.H.D.P.J. (2020). HR analytics: A literature review and new conceptual model. *International Journal of Scientific and Research Publications (IJSRP), 10*(6), 130-141.
[http://dx.doi.org/10.29322/IJSRP.10.06.2020.p10217]

CHAPTER 3

Predictive Analytics in Recruitment and Selection Practices

Sasirekha V.[1,*], **Nithyashree N.**[2] and **Sarulatha N.**[3]

[1] *Faculty of Management, SRM Institute of Science & Technology, Vadapalani, Chennai, India*

[2] *Sri Sairam Engineering College, Chennai, India*

[3] *Management Studies DG Vaishnava College, Chennai, India*

Abstract: Predictive analytics in recruitment and selection analytics in HR are increasingly important in a competitive job market. The importance of predictive measures in recruitment and selection analytics provides practical guidance for HR professionals looking to implement these measures in their organizations. Predictive measures involve the use of data-driven methods and statistical analyses to identify and hire the most qualified candidates for a given job. This approach relies on the collection and analysis of various data points, such as job requirements, candidate qualifications, and hiring outcomes, to develop models that predict which candidates are most likely to succeed in the role. By leveraging this information, HR professionals can streamline the recruitment process, reduce the risk of making hiring mistakes, and improve overall organizational performance. This article aims to provide the key predictive measures used in HR analytics to help organizations make better hiring decisions and an overview of key concepts and benefits associated with predictive measures in recruitment and selection analytics in HR, along with the challenges and limitations associated with the use of predictive measures in HR analytics and recommendations for overcoming these challenges.

Keywords: Predictive measures, Predictive analytics, Recruitment, Selection.

INTRODUCTION

Selection and recruitment play crucial roles in building a successful and capable workforce for an organization. Recruitment involves attracting and identifying potential candidates for job openings. This process includes creating job descriptions, advertising positions, sourcing candidates, and establishing a pool of potential hires. Effective recruitment ensures that the organization has access to a

* **Corresponding author Sasirekha V.:** Faculty of Management, SRM Institute of Science & Technology, Vadapalani, Chennai, India; E-mail: prof.sasirekha@gmail.com

Sandeep Kumar Kautish & Anuj Sheopuri (Eds.)

diverse and qualified talent pool from which to choose. Selection, on the other hand, is the process of evaluating and choosing the best-suited candidates from the pool generated during recruitment (Belizón, M.J. and Kieran, S., 2022). This involves assessing candidates' qualifications, skills, experience, and fit with the company culture. The goal of selection is to identify individuals who not only have the required skills but also align with the organization's values and can contribute positively to its goals.

The processes are interconnected and influence the overall success of an organization. An effective recruitment and selection strategy ensures that the right people are placed in the right roles, which leads to improved employee performance, reduced turnover, and a stronger organizational culture. It involves data analysis to predict the success and performance of candidates. This approach uses historical data to identify patterns and factors that correlate with job success, helping organizations make more informed hiring decisions. It can lead to more efficient and effective candidate screening, reduced bias, and improved overall hiring outcomes. Predictive analytics in recruitment and selection involves leveraging statistical algorithms to forecast which candidates are likely to perform well in a given role. By analyzing factors like past job performance, skills experience, and even behavioral traits, organizations can identify patterns that correlate with success (Angrave, D. *et al.*, 2016).

This approach helps HR professionals make data-driven decisions, enhance the quality of hires, and streamline the hiring process by focusing on candidates who have a higher likelihood of excelling in the role. Recruitment and selection are integral components of human resource management that focus on identifying, attracting, and hiring the most suitable candidates for specific job roles within an organization (Singh, A., Singh, H., and Singh, A., 2022). Recruitment involves the process of actively seeking and attracting potential candidates to apply for job openings. This process begins with defining the requirements of the job, creating compelling job descriptions, and then promoting these openings through various channels such as job boards, social media, career fairs, and company websites.

The goal is to generate a pool of diverse and qualified candidates who are interested in joining the organization. Selection, on the other hand, is the process of evaluating and choosing the best-fit candidates from the pool of applicants generated during recruitment. This involves assessing candidates' qualifications, skills, experience, and compatibility with the organization's culture and values. Selection methods can include interviews, assessments, reference checks, and background screenings. Together, the recruitment and selection process not only leads to higher job satisfaction and performance among employees but also contributes to building a strong and capable workforce that aligns with the organization's objectives (Dubey, R. *et al.*, 2019).

Understanding HR Analytics in Recruitment and Selection

HR analytics in recruitment and selection involves using data-driven approaches to gather insights, make informed decisions, and optimize the processes of attracting, evaluating, and hiring candidates. It involves using data and statistical analysis to enhance the hiring process. It helps in identifying trends, improving decision-making, and optimizing recruitment strategies based on factors like candidate sourcing, interview performance, and employee retention. By analyzing data, organizations can make more informed choices, reduce bias, and ultimately build stronger teams (Jabir, B., Falih, N. and Rahmani, K., 2019; Pessach, D., Singer *et al.*, 2020). Here is how HR analytics is applied in these areas:

Data Collection

HR analytics starts with collecting relevant data about candidates, including their skills, education, experience, and other attributes. This data is often collected through application forms, resumes, assessments, and other sources.

Candidate Sourcing

Analytics helps identify the most effective channels for candidate sourcing, such as job boards, social media platforms, or employee referrals, based on historical data and conversion rates.

Predictive Analytics

By analyzing historical data, organizations can predict future hiring needs and trends, enabling proactive talent acquisition planning.

Employee Retention

Analytics can highlight factors contributing to employee turnover, enabling strategies to improve retention and job satisfaction.

Diversity and Inclusion

Analytics can uncover biases in hiring processes, allowing organizations to address inequalities and promote diversity and inclusion.

Candidate Assessment

Analyzing interview and assessment data can help identify traits that correlate with successful employees, leading to more targeted evaluation and better hiring outcomes.

Employee Retention

Analytics can highlight factors contributing to employee turnover, enabling strategies to improve retention and job satisfaction.

Continuous Improvement

Regularly analyzing recruitment data allows organizations to refine their strategies and processes over time, optimizing results.

Overall, understanding HR analytics in recruitment and selection enhances the precision, efficiency, and fairness of hiring practices, leading to better-fit candidates and stronger teams.

Importance of Recruitment and Selection

Recruitment and selection are pivotal aspects of HR analytics because they play a crucial role in shaping an organization's workforce (Karim, M.M., Bhuiyan, M.Y.A., Nath *et al.*, 2021). Integrating analytics into these processes offers several important benefits:

Data-Driven Decision Making

Identify key metrics and performance indicators (KPIs) relevant to recruitment, such as time to fill, cost per hire, offer acceptance rate, and quality of hire. Gather relevant data from various sources, including applicant tracking system, interviews, assessments, and candidate feedback. Ensure data accuracy and consistency by cleaning, organizing, and structuring the data for analysis. Apply statistical methods and data visualization techniques to uncover patterns, correlations, and trends within the recruitment process. Analyze data, identify biases in the hiring process, and take corrective actions to ensure fair and unbiased selection.

Cost Management

The total cost associated with hiring a candidate, including advertising, agency fees, and interview expenses. Analytics can identify areas where costs can be reduced without compromising the quality of hire. To determine the recruitment channels yield the best candidates at the lowest cost. Allocate resources to the most effective channels and reduce spending on less productive ones. Analyze the source of successful hires and their associated costs. This helps focus efforts on the channels that provide the best return on investment.

Strategic Work Force Planning

Analyze the historical data to forecast future talent requirements based on growth projections, market trends, and business goals. Identify gaps between existing skills within the organization and the skills needed for future roles. Identify gaps between existing skills within the organization and the skills needed for future roles. Build talent pools of potential candidates for future positions based on skill sets, demographics, and market demand.

Enhancing Candidate Experience

Use analytics to assess the usability of the career website and application portal, ensuring an intuitive and user-friendly interface. Data feedback and data optimize email and communication templates, making them clear, informative, and engaging. Use data to streamline interview scheduling, reducing delays and ensuring a smooth experience for candidates. Gather and analyze candidate feedback to identify pain points, gather insights, and make necessary improvements.

Compliance and Legal Considerations

Ensure that candidate data is collected, stored, and processed in accordance with data protection regulations, such as GDPR, CCPA, or local data privacy laws. Use anonymization techniques when analyzing data to prevent the identification of individual candidates and to maintain confidentially. Maintain records of data processing activities, including analytics, to demonstrate compliance with legal requirements.

Key Aspects of Recruitment and Selection in HR Analytics

Recruitment and selection are critical HR processes that involve several key aspects to ensure the right candidates are chosen for job roles (Meena, M.R. and Parimalarani, G., 2019):

Job Analysis

Understanding the specific requirements, responsibilities, and qualifications of the position to create an accurate job description and candidate profile.

Sourcing

Identifying and attracting potential candidates through channels like job boards, social media, career fairs, and employee referrals.

Screening

Reviewing applications and resumes to shortlist candidates who meet the initial criteria, ensuring they have the necessary qualifications and experience.

Interviewing

Conducting interviews to assess the candidate's skills, competencies, and cultural fit with the organization.

Assessment

Administering tests, exercises, or simulations to evaluate candidate technical skills, cognitive abilities, and job-related traits.

Background Checks

Verifying the candidate's employment history, educational qualifications, and criminal records to ensure accuracy and honesty.

Reference Checks

Contacting provided references to gather insights into candidate's work habits, strengths, and areas for development.

Decision Making

Evaluating all collected information to make informed hiring decisions that align with the organization's goals and team dynamics.

Offer and Negotiation

Extending a job offer that includes compensation, benefits, and other terms, followed by negotiation if needed.

Onboarding

Integrating the new employee into the organization through orientation, training, and providing necessary resources.

Legal Compliance

Ensuring the entire process adheres to labor laws, anti-discrimination regulations, and equal employment opportunity guidelines.

Diversity and Inclusion

Ensuring that the recruitment and selection process promotes diversity and inclusion, aiming for a balanced and representative workforce.

Feedback and Improvement

Regularly assessing the recruitment and selection processes and gathering feedback from stakeholders to make continuous improvements.

Employer Branding

Presenting the organization in a positive light to attract top talent and maintain a strong reputation in the job market.

Technology Integration

Using advanced tools such as applicant tracking systems, data analytics, and AI-driven assessments to streamline and enhance the process.

Candidate Experience

Focusing on providing a positive experience for candidates throughout the process, regardless of the outcome.

These aspects collectively ensure that the recruitment and selection process is thorough, fair, and effective in identifying candidates who will contribute positively to the organization.

Methods of Recruitment and Selection in HR Analytics

HR analytics can enhance various methods of recruitment and selection by providing data-driven insights to improve decision-making (Kremer, K., 2018; McCartney, S. and Fu, N., 2022). Some methods are:

Job Posting and Job Boards

Analytics can help identify which job boards or platforms yield the highest quality candidates based on conversion rates and applicant demographics.

Social Media Recruitment

Analytics can track engagement and conversion rates from different social media channels, helping to focus efforts on platforms where potential candidates are most active.

Employee Referrals

Analytics can measure the success of referrals, helping to refine referral programs and identify employees who consistently refer strong candidates.

Recruitment Agencies

Analytics can assess the performance of different agencies in terms of candidate quality, time-to-fill, and cost, aiding in agency selection.

Predictive Hiring Models

Utilizing historical data, analytics can develop models that predict which candidates are most likely to succeed based on past hires with similar attributes.

Behavioral Assessments

Analytics can analyze assessment data to identify traits and behaviors that correlate with high-performing employees, guiding assessment criteria.

Video Interviews

Analytics can review video interview performance and assess how well a candidate's responses align with desired competencies.

Resume Screening

Machine learning can be used to screen resumes, identifying keywords and experience that match the job description.

Talent Pipelining

Analytics can help in identifying and nurturing potential candidates who might be a fit for future roles, based on their past interactions and engagement.

Diversity Hiring

Analytics can track the diversity of applicant pools and highlight potential biases in the selection process, aiding in creating more inclusive hiring strategies.

Candidate Experience Analysis

Analytics can evaluate candidate feedback and sentiment throughout the recruitment process to identify areas for improvement.

Time-to-Fill and Cost-Per-Hire Analysis

Analytics can track the time taken to fill positions and the associated costs, helping to optimize the recruitment process for efficiency and cost-effectiveness.

Exit Interviewing Analysis

By analyzing data from exit interviews, analytics can identify recurring reasons for turnover, guiding improvements in the selection process to reduce attrition.

HR analytics can provide valuable insights into each stage of the recruitment and selection process, enabling data-driven decisions that lead to better outcomes and more effective talent acquisition strategies.

Implementation of HR Analytics in Recruitment And Selection

Implementing recruitment and selection with HR analytics involves a systematic approach to leverage data for smarter decision-making:

Define Objective

Clearly outline your recruitment and selection goals. Identify what key metrics need to be improved or optimized using analytics.

Data Collection

Gather relevant data from various sources such as applicant tracking systems, HR databases, interview assessments, and performance reviews.

Data Integration

Centralize the collected data in a unified system or data warehouse for easy access and analysis.

Data Cleaning

Ensure data accuracy and consistency by cleaning and organizing the data and resolving any discrepancies or missing information.

Data Analysis

Apply statistical analysis and data visualization techniques to extract insights from the data. This could involve identifying trends, patterns, and correlations.

Choose Analytics Tools

Select appropriate analytics tools or platforms that suit your needs, whether they are Excel, specialized HR analytics software, or more advanced machine learning tools.

Identify Key Metrics

Determine the key performance indicators (KPI) that need to be measured, such as time-to-fill, cost-per-hire, quality of hire, diversity metrics, and candidate sourcing effectiveness.

Identify Improvement Areas

Use analytics to pinpoint bottlenecks, areas of bias, or inefficiencies in the recruitment process that could be addressed.

Continuous Monitoring

Set up a system for ongoing monitoring of recruitment and selection data to track changes over time and adapt strategies accordingly.

Feedback Loop

Collaborate with hiring managers, recruiters, and stakeholders to incorporate their insights and feedback into the analysis process.

Actionable Insights

Translate data insights into actionable strategies; for example, if analytics reveal a particular assessment is correlated with high-performing employees, adjust the selection process.

A/B Testing

Experiment with different recruitment strategies and evaluate their impact through A/B testing, using analytics to determine which approach yields better results.

Training

Provide training to HR professionals and hiring managers on how to interpret and use analytics effectively to make informed decisions.

Reporting

Create regular reports and dashboards that visualize the recruitment and selection analytics, making it easier for stakeholders to understand and act upon the insights.

Iterative and Improve

Regularly review the impact of analytics-driven strategies, refine your approach based on results, and continue to innovate.

Overall, implementing HR analytics in recruitment and selection is an iterative process that requires collaboration, adaptability, and a commitment to using data to drive positive changes in hiring practices.

Key Indicators of Recruitment and Selection in HR Analytics

Time to Hire

The time between posting the job opening and the first applicant submitting their application. The time taken to review applications, shortlist candidates, and identify those who meet the basic qualifications. The time spent scheduling, conducting, and completing interviews with the shortlisted candidates. The time it takes for the hiring team to evaluate interview feedback, discuss candidates, and make a final decision. The time needed to prepare the job offer, including salary negotiation and drafting the employment contract. The time from when the offer is extended to the candidate's acceptance.

Quality of Hire

The new hires perform their job tasks, meet or exceed expectations, and contribute to the team and organization's goals. Measure the output and efficiency of the new hire in their role. Assess whether the new hire possesses the skills, competencies, and qualifications necessary for their role as outlined in the job description. Determine whether the new hire aligns with the company's culture, values, and work environment, which can impact their long-term success. A higher retention rate usually indicates a better quality of hire. Gather feedback from managers to gauge the new hire's ability to collaborate, communicate, and contribute to the team.

Applicant-To-Interview Ratio

It is a recruitment metric that represents the number of applicants who progress to the interview stage of the hiring process. It provides insights into the effectiveness of your initial screening and candidate qualification processes. It divides the number of applicants who are invited for an interview by the total number of applicants for a particular job opening. The resulting ratio reflects the proportion of candidates who successfully move from the application stage to the interview stage.

Interview-To-Offer Ratio

It measures the proportion of candidates who are extended a job offer after they have participated in interviews. This ratio provides insights into the selection of your interview process and how effectively you are converting interviews into actual job offers. To calculate the interview-to-offer ratio, divide the number of candidates who receive job offers by the total number of candidates who were interviewed for a specific job opening. The resulting ratio indicates the percentage of interviewed candidates who were deemed suitable for employment and received an offer.

Time spent in each hiring stage

The time taken to review and screen incoming applications to identify candidates who meet the basic qualifications. The time spent conducting phone or video screenings to further evaluate candidates fit for the position. The time required to coordinate and schedule interviews with candidates and interviewers and classify interviews into one-on-one panel interviews or assessment-based interviews. The duration taken by interviewers and hiring managers to assess interview performance and discuss potential candidates. The time allocated to contacting references and conducting background checks to verify candidates' information. The period from offer acceptance to the candidate's first day of work, involving orientation, paperwork, and initial training.

Future Trends

The future of recruitment and selection in HR analytics is promising and holds several trends that are expected to shape the field (Marler, J. & Boudreau, J., 2017). Some key trends are:

Predictive Analytics

HR analytics will increasingly leverage predictive models to forecast future hiring needs and identify the most suitable candidates. This involves analyzing historical data to anticipate workforce requirements and proactively source talent.

AI-Powered Automation

Artificial Intelligence (AI) and Machine Learning (ML) will continue to automate routine tasks in recruitment, such as resume screening, interview scheduling, and candidate communication. This streamline processes and allows HR professionals to focus on higher-value tasks.

Real-Time Data Analysis

Real-time analytics will become more prevalent, allowing HR teams to make faster decisions. This can be particularly useful during high-volume hiring periods or when adapting to rapidly changing market conditions.

Video and Social Media Analytics

Analyzing video interviews and social media profiles can provide deeper insights into candidates' personalities, communication skills, and cultural fit, helping to make more informed hiring decisions.

Integrated HR Technology Platforms

The integration of different HR technology platforms will become more seamless, enabling data sharing and analysis across the entire employee lifecycle.

Overall, the integration of analytics in recruitment and selection processes will lead to more data-driven, efficient, and strategic hiring decisions, contributing to the success of an organization.

CONCLUSION

In conclusion, the integration of HR analytics into the recruitment and selection process is a significant evolution in talent acquisition strategies. This data-driven approach has revolutionized the way organizations identify, assess, and hire candidates. By harnessing the power of advanced analytics, organizations can make more informed and strategic decisions, ultimately leading to improved hiring outcomes and workforce success. Data-driven insights enable HR professionals to make objective decisions based on evidence rather than relying solely on intuition. Automation and predictive models streamline processes, reducing time-to-fill positions and freeing up HR resources for more strategic tasks. Ensuring the ethical use of data and addressing potential biases in algorithms are crucial to maintaining fairness and transparency in the process. HR professionals need to develop analytical skills to effectively interpret and utilize data for decision-making. Reliable and accurate data is essential for meaningful analysis. Organizations need robust data collection and management practices. While automation enhances efficiency, maintaining a human touch in interactions with candidates remains important for a positive candidate experience. Integrating various HR systems and sharing data seamlessly can be a complex endeavor. Analytics enable organizations to assess the effectiveness of recruitment strategies and make adjustments for ongoing improvements. In a rapidly evolving job market, where talent is a competitive advantage, the role of HR analytics in recruitment and selection will continue to expand. As organizations refine their analytical capabilities and adopt innovative technologies, they will be better equipped to identify and engage a top talent, align their workforce with strategic goals, and drive sustainable success in the dynamic business landscape.

REFERENCES

Angrave, D., Charlwood, A., Kirkpatrick, I., Lawrence, M., Stuart, M. (2016). HR and analytics: why HR is set to fail the big data challenge. *Hum. Resour. Manage. J., 26*(1), 1-11.
[http://dx.doi.org/10.1111/1748-8583.12090]

Belizón, M.J., Kieran, S. (2022). Human resources analytics: A legitimacy process. *Hum. Resour. Manage. J., 32*(3), 603-630.
[http://dx.doi.org/10.1111/1748-8583.12417]

Dubey, R., Gunasekaran, A., Childe, S.J., Papadopoulos, T., Luo, Z., Wamba, S.F., Roubaud, D. (2019). Can big data and predictive analytics improve social and environmental sustainability? *Technol. Forecast. Soc. Change, 144*, 534-545.
[http://dx.doi.org/10.1016/j.techfore.2017.06.020]

Jabir, B., Falih, N., Rahmani, K. (2019). HR analytics a roadmap for decision making: case study. *Indonesian Journal of Electrical Engineering and Computer Science, 15*(2), 979-990.
[http://dx.doi.org/10.11591/ijeecs.v15.i2.pp979-990]

Karim, M.M., Bhuiyan, M.Y.A., Nath, S.K.D., Latif, W.B. (2021). Conceptual Framework of Recruitment and Selection Process. *International Journal of Business and Social Research, 11*(02), 18-25.

Kremer, K. (2018). HR analytics and its moderating factors. *Vezetéstudomány-Budapest Management Review, 49*(11), 62-68.

Marler, J.H., Boudreau, J.W. (2017). An evidence-based review of HR Analytics. *Int. J. Hum. Resour. Manage., 28*(1), 3-26.
[http://dx.doi.org/10.1080/09585192.2016.1244699]

McCartney, S., Fu, N. (2022). Bridging the gap: why, how and when HR analytics can impact organizational performance. *Manage. Decis., 60*(13), 25-47.
[http://dx.doi.org/10.1108/MD-12-2020-1581]

Meena, M.R., Parimalarani, G. (2019). Human capital analytics: A game changer for hr professionals. *International Journal of Recent Technology and Engineering., 8*, 3963-3965.

Pessach, D., Singer, G., Avrahami, D., Chalutz Ben-Gal, H., Shmueli, E., Ben-Gal, I. (2020). Employees recruitment: A prescriptive analytics approach *via* machine learning and mathematical programming. *Decis.*

Support Syst., 134, 113290.
[http://dx.doi.org/10.1016/j.dss.2020.113290] [PMID: 32501316]

Singh, A., Singh, H., Singh, A. (2022). People Analytics: Augmenting Horizon from Predictive Analytics to Prescriptive Analytics. *Decision Intelligence Analytics and the Implementation of Strategic Business Management.* (pp. 145-153). Cham: Springer.
[http://dx.doi.org/10.1007/978-3-030-82763-2_13]

HR Analytics and People Management

Sasirekha V.[1,*], **Abinash T.**[2] and **Venkateswara Prasad B.**[3]

[1] *Faculty of Management, SRM Institute of Science & Technology, Vadapalani, Chennai, India*

[2] *Sri Sairam Engineering College, Chennai, India*

[3] *Management Studies, Sri Sairam Engineering College, Chennai, India*

Abstract: Human resource (HR) analytics is a crucial part of people management, which aids businesses in making decisions about their human resources. The goal of HR analytics is to increase employee engagement, retention rates, performance management, and hiring procedures by using data analysis methods and technologies to better understand workforce trends and patterns. Recent developments in HR analytics highlight the value of predictive analysis for workforce planning and management, including AI and ML, for decision-making while also placing a strong emphasis on data protection, security, and ethics. Among the many functions that HR analytics may play in people management is improving the hiring procedure. By examining important characteristics like education level or job experience, data-driven insights can assist in selecting potential candidates who are most likely to succeed inside the organization. Given that it enables companies to foresee future staffing demands based on current market conditions or demographic shifts, recent trends indicate that predictive analysis will continue to play a crucial role in workforce planning and management. As a result, human resource professionals may use cutting-edge technology to gain important insights into how their teams work, enabling them to build more effective and productive teams.

Keywords: Future trends, Human resource analytics, HR analytics implementation, KPI, Metrics, People management, Workforce trends, Workforce patterns.

INTRODUCTION

In the ever-evolving landscape of contemporary business, the role of human resources (HR) has transcended its traditional administrative boundaries. Today, HR is at the forefront of strategic decision-making, and this transformation is driven by HR analytics. In recent years, HR analytics has surged in importance,

* Corresponding author Sasirekha V.: Faculty of Management, SRM Institute of Science & Technology, Vadapalani, Chennai, India; E-mail: prof.sasirekha@gmail.com

Sandeep Kumar Kautish & Anuj Sheopuri (Eds.)

leveraging data-driven insights to shape the way organizations function. With technology enabling the collection, analysis, and interpretation of vast amounts of HR data, organizations now have the tools to make more informed and precise decisions concerning talent acquisition, performance evaluation, and employee engagement. These analytics not only offer a glimpse into the past and present but also illuminate potential future trends and challenges. The role of HR analytics in people management explores the dynamic landscape of HR analytics and its pivotal role in contemporary people management (Marler J H and Boudreau J.W., 2019).

In today's dynamic and competitive business environment, effective people management is a crucial factor for organizations striving to maintain a competitive edge. Human resources (HR) professionals play a vital role in ensuring that the organization's workforce is engaged, productive, and strategically aligned with the overall goals and objectives. HR analytics, also known as people analytics, has emerged as a powerful tool in modern-day people management (Marler J.H. and Boudreau J.W., 2020). It entails gathering, analyzing, and interpreting HR-related data in order to acquire insights into various elements of the workforce. By leveraging data-driven approaches, HR analytics enables organizations to make informed decisions, optimize processes, and drive positive outcomes in managing their people.

The role of HR analytics in people management is multifaceted. It supports organizations in talent acquisition, where data-driven hiring practices help identify the right candidates with the desired skills and cultural fit. It also plays a pivotal role in talent retention, as HR analytics enables organizations to gain insights into employee satisfaction, identify potential flight risks, and develop targeted strategies to enhance employee engagement and satisfaction. Furthermore, HR analytics facilitates effective performance management by tracking and analyzing employee performance metrics, identifying areas for improvement, and aligning individual goals with organizational objectives. It aids in workforce planning by analyzing data on turnover rates, succession planning, and identifying skill gaps to ensure the organization has the right talent in place for future needs (Van den Heuvel S., Bondarouk T., and Strohmeier S., 2020).

Additionally, HR analytics contributes to learning and development initiatives by identifying skill development needs, monitoring training effectiveness, and evaluating the impact of learning interventions on employee performance. It also enables HR professionals to measure the ROI of their initiatives and make data-driven decisions. Overall, HR analytics provides HR professionals with the necessary insights to drive evidence-based decision making, enhance operational efficiency, and align people management strategies with the organization's goals

(Rasmussen, T., and D. Ulrich, 2020). Organizations can unleash the full potential of their workforce and achieve a competitive edge in today's fast-developing business landscape by using the power of data and analytics.

Understanding HR Analytics

HR analytics is a transformational field within human resources management that focuses on the systematic gathering, analysis, and interpretation of data to inform HR decision-making. It has grown dramatically in recent years, spurred by technological breakthroughs and a rising acknowledgment of its potential to improve people management practices. HR has always been concerned with administrative chores, compliance, and employee relations. However, as businesses strive to become more agile and data-driven, HR analytics has gained prominence by enabling HR professionals to transition from reactive to proactive roles (GitikaTalukdar, 2016). One core concept in HR analytics is the distinction between various analytics levels:

Descriptive Analytics

This involves the examination of historical data to understand past HR trends and events. It forms the foundation for more advanced analytics and helps HR professionals identify patterns and areas that require attention. For example, it can be used to track employee turnover rates over time.

Diagnostic Analytics

Building on descriptive analytics, this level aims to uncover the root causes of HR challenges or trends. It involves digging deeper into data to answer "why" questions. For instance, it can help HR managers understand why certain departments experience higher turnover rates.

Predictive Analytics

This level takes HR analytics into the future by using statistical models and machine learning algorithms to forecast HR trends and issues. For instance, it can predict which employees are at risk of leaving the organization based on historical data and current behavior.

Prescriptive Analytics

The most advanced level, prescriptive analytics, goes beyond predicting outcomes to recommend actions. It provides HR professionals with actionable insights on how to address HR challenges or capitalize on opportunities effectively. For example, it can suggest personalized retention strategies for employees identified as high-risk.

Recent advancements in data analytics technologies, including artificial intelligence and natural language processing, have further enhanced HR analytics capabilities. HR departments may use these technologies to swiftly analyze enormous datasets, extract valuable insights, and automate repetitive operations, allowing HR experts to focus on more strategic objectives. Furthermore, HR analytics has extended its reach beyond traditional HR functions. It now plays a pivotal role in various aspects of people management, including talent acquisition, workforce planning, diversity and inclusion initiatives, and employee experience enhancement. For example, organizations are increasingly using analytics to optimize recruitment processes, ensuring that they attract and retain top talent. Eventually, HR analytics represents a paradigm shift in how HR professionals approach their roles. By harnessing the power of data, organizations can make evidence-based decisions, tailor HR strategies to individual employee needs, and ultimately create more engaged and productive workforces.

The Importance of People Management

In today's dynamic and competitive business landscape, organizations are recognizing that their most valuable asset is not their products, services, or technologies—it is their people. Effective people management has emerged as a strategic imperative for organizations seeking to thrive in an era characterized by rapid change, globalization, and technological disruption. At its core, people management encompasses all the activities, processes, and strategies involved in acquiring, developing, retaining, and optimizing a workforce. This multifaceted discipline encompasses HR functions like recruitment, training and development, performance evaluation, employee engagement, and workforce planning. Its significance has grown exponentially as businesses recognize that talent can be a key differentiator in a crowded marketplace. Several factors underscore the critical importance of People Management:

Talent as a Competitive Advantage

In a knowledge-based economy, the skills, expertise, and creativity of employees are critical for innovation and sustained competitive advantage. Businesses that excel in attracting, nurturing, and retaining top talent are more likely to outperform their competitors.

Employee Productivity

Effective people management enhances employee productivity and performance. When employees feel valued, are given opportunities for growth, and have their well-being prioritized, they tend to be more engaged and motivated, resulting in higher productivity levels.

Employee Retention

High turnover can be costly and disruptive. Organizations that invest in People Management strategies aimed at retaining employees can save substantial resources while maintaining stability and expertise within the workforce.

Adaptability to Change

Businesses are constantly facing changes, whether it's shifts in market dynamics, technology disruptions, or global crises like the recent pandemic. People Management practices that foster a culture of agility and resilience are vital for navigating such challenges.

Employee Experience

The employee experience is a crucial factor in attracting and retaining talent. Organizations that prioritize creating a positive work environment, providing growth opportunities, and ensuring work-life balance tend to have higher employee satisfaction and retention rates.

Given these considerations, modern organizations are reimagining their HR departments as strategic partners rather than just administrative functions. They recognize the need for HR to be forward-thinking, data-driven, and closely aligned with organizational goals. This shift is where HR analytics comes into play. HR analytics empowers organizations to make evidence-based decisions about their workforce, aligning HR strategies with overall business objectives. By analyzing data on employee performance, engagement, turnover, and other critical HR metrics, organizations can identify areas for improvement, allocate resources more efficiently, and develop strategies to enhance the overall employee experience.

Furthermore, HR analytics can help organizations identify patterns and trends in their workforce data, providing insights into areas such as talent acquisition, workforce planning, and succession management. For instance, analytics can reveal which recruitment channels yield the best hires, allowing organizations to focus their resources on the most effective methods. In a nutshell, people management is no longer a peripheral HR function but a core driver of organizational success. In an environment where attracting, retaining, and developing top talent is paramount, businesses must recognize the pivotal role of effective people management in achieving their strategic goals. HR analytics is a critical tool in this pursuit, enabling organizations to harness the power of data to optimize their people management practices.

Integration of Hr Analytics

In the ever-evolving landscape of human resource management, the integration of HR analytics has emerged as a transformative force. This integration is reshaping the way organizations approach people management, enabling HR professionals to move beyond traditional practices and become strategic partners in driving business success (Falletta, S.V. and Combs, W.L., 2021). At its core, the integration of HR analytics involves the seamless incorporation of data-driven insights into HR decision-making processes.

Optimizing Talent Acquisition

One of the key areas where HR analytics is making a significant impact is talent acquisition. Organizations may make better-informed decisions regarding recruiting efforts by utilizing data and analytics. This involves determining the most efficient sourcing routes, refining job descriptions based on data-backed insights, and even predicting which candidates are most likely to succeed in specific roles. For instance, organizations can analyze historical hiring data to determine which sources, such as job boards or employee referrals, have yielded the highest-quality hires. By concentrating their efforts on the most successful channels, organizations can improve the efficiency and effectiveness of their recruitment processes, ultimately reducing time-to-fill and cost-per-hire. Furthermore, HR analytics enables the development of predictive models that assess a candidate's fit for a particular role. These models can take into account factors such as skills, experience, and cultural alignment, helping organizations identify top candidates early in the recruitment process. This predictive capability significantly enhances the quality of hires, reducing turnover rates and ensuring a better talent fit.

Enhancing Performance Management

Performance management is another critical area where HR analytics is driving change. Traditional performance reviews, conducted annually or semi-annually, often suffer from subjectivity and a lack of actionable insights. HR analytics addresses these challenges by enabling continuous performance monitoring and feedback. Through real-time data analysis, organizations can track employee performance metrics, identify areas for improvement, and provide timely feedback. For example, dashboards that display key performance indicators (KPIs) can help managers and employees alike visualize performance trends and take corrective actions as needed. Moreover, HR analytics can support the development of predictive models that forecast future performance. By analyzing historical data on factors such as training, feedback, and engagement, organizations can identify predictors of high performance and use this information to proactively develop employees' skills and capabilities.

Workforce Planning and Succession Management

A successful workforce strategy is essential for ensuring that an organization has the proper personnel in place to meet its strategic objectives. HR analytics plays a pivotal role in this process by providing insights into current workforce capabilities and identifying future talent needs. For instance, organizations can analyze employee skills data to determine where skill gaps exist within the workforce. Armed with this information, they can implement targeted training and development programs to bridge these gaps and ensure a pipeline of skilled talent for critical roles. Additionally, HR analytics can assist in succession planning by identifying high-potential employees within the organization. By evaluating factors such as performance, leadership abilities, and career progression, organizations can proactively nurture and prepare individuals for key leadership positions, reducing the risk of leadership gaps during transitions.

Employee Participation and Preservation

Employee involvement and retention are perennial organizational concerns. High turnover rates may be costly and disruptive, making it critical to identify and solve attrition-related problems. HR analytics enables organizations to analyze employee engagement survey data and identify drivers of engagement or disengagement. For example, by correlating survey responses with various HR metrics, organizations can uncover patterns that reveal which aspects of work are most closely tied to employee satisfaction. Furthermore, predictive analytics can be employed to forecast employee turnover. By analyzing historical turnover data and identifying common factors leading to attrition, organizations can create early warning systems that flag individuals at risk of leaving. Armed with this information, HR can intervene with targeted retention strategies, such as career development opportunities or adjustments to compensation packages.

Strategic Decision-Making

Ultimately, the integration of HR analytics enables HR professionals to become strategic partners within their organizations. By providing data-driven insights, HR can contribute to broader business strategies and goals. For instance, HR analytics can assist in workforce cost optimization. By analyzing compensation data and benchmarking it against industry standards, organizations can ensure they are offering competitive compensation packages while maintaining cost efficiency. Moreover, HR analytics can contribute to diversity and inclusion initiatives. By tracking diversity metrics and analyzing patterns, organizations can identify areas where diversity may be lacking and develop strategies to foster inclusivity and representation. In essence, the integration of HR analytics elevates HR's role from an administrative function to a strategic one.

Metrics and Key Performance Indicators (KPIs) In People Management

In the realm of people management, the ability to measure and assess various aspects of the workforce is paramount. Metrics and key performance indicators (KPIs) serve as the compass guiding HR professionals toward informed decision making, strategy formulation, and continuous improvement (Gabčanová Iveta, 2012). These metrics offer quantifiable insights into HR processes, employee performance, and the overall health of the workforce, facilitating the alignment of HR strategies with organizational objectives.

Talent Acquisition Metrics

Talent acquisition is the first step in effective people management. Metrics in this area focus on optimizing the recruitment process to attract and select top talent efficiently. Common talent acquisition metrics include:

Period-to-Fill

The amount of time it takes to fill a job opening from the time it is posted.

Cost-per-Hire

Assesses costs of the recruiting process, such as advertising, interviewing, and onboarding.

Quality of Hire

Assesses the success and performance of hires in relation to their qualifications and job fit.

These metrics enable organizations to refine their hiring strategies, reduce recruitment costs, and ensure they are bringing in candidates who align with the company's values and goals.

Employee Engagement and Satisfaction Metrics

Employee engagement and satisfaction are crucial for retaining talent and fostering a positive work environment. Metrics in this category aim to quantify employee sentiment and identify areas for improvement. The following are key metrics:

Employee Net Promoter Rating (eNPR)

The propensity of employees to recommend the organization as a place to work.

Employee Satisfaction Score

Evaluates overall employee contentment through regular surveys.

Engagement Index

Assesses employee commitment and motivation.

These metrics help HR professionals gauge the effectiveness of employee engagement initiatives and address potential issues affecting morale.

Performance Management Metrics

Performance management metrics are instrumental in evaluating employee productivity and effectiveness. They include:

Performance Appraisal Ratings

Measures employee performance based on evaluations by supervisors.

Goal Attainment

Assesses the extent to which employees meet their performance objectives (360-Degree).

Feedback Scores

Gathers input on employee performance from multiple sources.

Training and Development Metrics

Learning and development are essential components of employee growth and skill enhancement. Metrics in this area assess the efficacy of training programs and suggest areas for improvement. Metrics that are relevant include:

Training ROI

Evaluates the return on investment in training initiatives.

Training Completion Rates

Measure the percentage of employees who successfully complete training programs.

Skills Gap Analysis

Identifies discrepancies between desired and actual employee skills.

Diversity and Inclusion Metrics

Diversity and inclusion are increasingly critical aspects of people management. Metrics in this category assess diversity representation and inclusion efforts. Key metrics include:

Diversity Index

Quantifies the degree of diversity within the organization, including gender, ethnicity, and age.

Inclusion Score

Measures employee perceptions of the organization's inclusivity efforts. These metrics assist in tracking progress toward diversity and inclusion goals and addressing disparities within the workforce.

Implementing HR Analytics in Organizations

Embracing HR analytics is a transformative journey that requires careful planning, strategic alignment, and a dedication to data-driven decision-making. (Lijun Wang, Yu Zhou *et al.*, 2024). While the advantages of HR analytics are numerous, the process of implementation can be complex. Here are key steps to effectively integrate HR analytics into an organization:

Leadership Buy-In

Begin with securing leadership support. Top-level executives should understand the value of HR analytics in achieving business goals. Their endorsement provides the necessary resources and organizational commitment for a successful implementation.

Data Infrastructure

Invest in robust data infrastructure. Ensure that data sources (HRIS, performance management systems, *etc.*) are integrated and capable of generating real-time data. Data quality and security are paramount.

Data Governance

Establish clear data governance policies to maintain data accuracy and compliance with privacy regulations. This includes defining who has access to data, data storage, and data retention policies.

Skills and Training

HR teams should possess the necessary analytical skills or receive training to effectively use analytics tools. Data literacy is crucial for understanding and interpreting HR data.

Identify Key Metrics

Determine which HR metrics and KPIs align with organizational objectives. This ensures that HR analytics efforts remain focused and actionable.

Select Analytics Tools

Choose analytics tools and software that suit the organization's needs and budget. These tools should support data visualization, predictive analytics, and reporting.

Implementing HR analytics is a dynamic process that evolves with the organization's needs and capabilities. Organizations may leverage the potential of HR analytics to optimize people management, enhance employee experiences, and drive overall company performance by following these steps and maintaining a commitment to data-driven decision-making.

CASE STUDIES

Case Study 1: Google Inc.

Google, known for its innovative culture, has harnessed HR analytics to enhance its people management practices. The tech giant employs a data-driven approach to recruit, develop, and retain top talent. Google's use of HR analytics is exemplified by its hiring process. By analyzing vast amounts of applicant data, Google has identified specific attributes and qualities that correlate with high-performing employees. This data-driven approach enables Google to make more informed hiring decisions, resulting in a workforce that is better aligned with the company's goals. Moreover, Google uses HR analytics to improve employee engagement. Through regular employee surveys and sentiment analysis, the company gauges the overall satisfaction of its workforce. The insights gained from these surveys help Google identify trends and areas for improvement, enabling the HR team to develop targeted programs and initiatives to enhance employee well-being and productivity.

Case Study 2: IBM

IBM, a global technology and consulting company, has successfully integrated HR analytics into its talent management strategies. IBM's HR team utilizes predictive analytics to identify employees at risk of leaving the company. By analyzing historical data and factors such as job satisfaction, compensation, and career progression, IBM can proactively intervene with retention strategies. This proactive approach has helped the company reduce turnover rates and retain valuable talent. Additionally, IBM applies HR analytics to workforce planning. Through workforce analytics, the company assesses current and future talent needs. This allows IBM to efficiently allocate resources, build talent pipelines, and ensure that the organization has the required talents in place to accomplish its strategic objectives.

Case Study 3: Hilton Worldwide

Hilton Worldwide, a global hospitality company, has embraced HR analytics to enhance its talent acquisition and employee engagement efforts. The company uses data analytics to optimize its recruitment process, including identifying the most effective hiring sources and evaluating the success of its recruitment marketing campaigns. By analyzing applicant data, Hilton can make data-driven decisions about which candidates are most likely to succeed in various roles, improving the quality of hires. Furthermore, Hilton leverages HR analytics to enhance the employee experience. The company collects and analyzes employee feedback and engagement data through surveys and sentiment analysis. These data help Hilton to adjust its employee programs and initiatives to the different requirements and preferences of its staff, resulting in higher employee satisfaction and retention rates. These case studies demonstrate how organizations across different industries have successfully implemented HR analytics to optimize their people management practices. By leveraging data-driven insights, these companies have improved talent acquisition, employee engagement, and retention, ultimately contributing to their overall success and competitive advantage.

FUTURE TRENDS IN HR ANALYTICS

As the field of HR analytics continues to evolve, several emerging trends are poised to shape the future of people management (Rasmussen, T., Ulrich, D., 2015). These trends leverage advancements in technology, increased data accessibility, and a growing recognition of the strategic importance of HR within organizations.

AI and Machine Learning Integration

AI and machine learning will play an increasingly prominent role in HR analytics. These technologies can analyze vast datasets to uncover hidden patterns and predict future HR trends. For example, AI-driven algorithms can help identify high-potential employees, forecast turnover risks, and recommend personalized learning and development paths.

Predictive Workforce Analytics

HR departments will move beyond reactive approaches to predictive workforce preparation. Organizations may estimate future talent demands and solve skill shortages and workforce imbalances by analyzing historical and real-time data. This enables better alignment of HR strategies with broader business objectives.

Employee Experience Enhancement

HR analytics will focus on enhancing the employee experience. Organizations will utilize data-driven insights to create more personalized and inclusive workplaces. By understanding employee preferences and needs, HR can tailor benefits, career paths, and development opportunities, resulting in higher employee satisfaction and retention.

Real-time Data Analytics

The shift toward real-time analytics will become more pronounced. Organizations will use data dashboards and analytics tools to monitor workforce trends and employee sentiment in real time.

Ethical and Responsible AI

With increased reliance on AI in HR, ethical considerations and responsible AI practices will gain importance. Organizations will need to ensure that AI algorithms are transparent, free from bias, and comply with data privacy regulations. Ethical AI practices will help maintain trust between employees and employers.

People Analytics Centers of Excellence

Organizations will establish dedicated People Analytics Centers of Excellence to centralize HR analytics expertise. These centers will serve as hubs for data analysis, research, and strategic guidance, ensuring a consistent and data-driven approach to people management.

Employee Well-being Metrics

Employee well-being will be a focal point of HR analytics. Metrics related to mental health, work-life balance, and overall well-being will be integrated into HR data analysis. These insights will guide initiatives aimed at improving employee wellness and productivity.

Continuous Learning and Upskilling

HR analytics will increasingly support continuous learning and upskilling efforts. By analyzing skill gaps and emerging industry trends, organizations can design targeted training programs that equip employees with the skills needed to adapt to evolving job roles.

The future of HR analytics is marked by technological advancements, a deepened commitment to employee well-being, and a more strategic role for HR within organizations. These emerging trends will enable HR professionals to harness the power of data and analytics to not only manage their people effectively but also to drive innovation, adapt to changing workforce dynamics, and achieve sustainable business success.

CONCLUSION

HR analytics has emerged as a game-changer, propelling HR from a traditional role to a strategic driver of organizational success. This has explored the multifaceted realm of HR analytics, emphasizing its pivotal role in modern HR practices. HR analytics offers a pathway to harness the power of data, enabling HR professionals to make evidence-based decisions across various facets of people management. The understanding of HR analytics, from descriptive insights to predictive models, provides organizations with the tools to optimize talent acquisition, enhance performance management, facilitate effective workforce planning, and foster employee engagement. It empowers HR departments to identify high-potential employees, predict turnover risks, and align HR strategies with broader business objectives. Looking ahead, the future of HR analytics promises even greater advancements. Artificial intelligence and machine learning will further augment HR decision-making, while a focus on ethics and responsible

AI will ensure transparency and fairness. Real-time data analytics will enable organizations to respond swiftly to workforce dynamics, and employee well-being metrics will become central to HR strategies. In this era of data-driven HR, organizations must recognize that their most valuable asset is their people. By embracing HR analytics, organizations can navigate the complexities of the modern workforce, respond to evolving talent needs, and foster a culture of continuous improvement. Ultimately, HR analytics is not merely a tool but a transformative force that empowers organizations to optimize their people management practices, enhance employee experiences, and ultimately achieve sustainable business success. As the role of HR analytics continues to evolve, its significance in shaping the future of people management cannot be underestimated, making it an indispensable asset for organizations committed to staying at the forefront of HR excellence.

REFERENCES

Falletta, S.V., Combs, W.L. (2021). The HR analytics cycle: a seven-step process for building evidence-based and ethical HR analytics capabilities. *J. Work-Appl. Manag., 13*(1), 51-68.
[http://dx.doi.org/10.1108/JWAM-03-2020-0020]

Gabcanova, I. (2012). Human Resources Key Performance Indicators. *Journal of Competitiveness, 4*(1), 117-128.
[http://dx.doi.org/10.7441/joc.2012.01.09]

(2016). Human Resources Analytics: An Approach towards Business Intelligence. *Int. J. Comput. Sci. Eng., 04*(07)

Lijun Wang, Yu Zhou *et al.* (2024). Determinants of effective HR analytics Implementation: An In-Depth review and a dynamic framework for future research. Journal of Business Research.
[http://dx.doi.org/10.1016/j.jbusres.2023.114312]

Marler, J.H., Boudreau, J.W. (2019). A substantiation-based examination of HR Analytics. *Int. J. Hum. Resour. Manage., 30*(1), 3-26.
[http://dx.doi.org/10.1080/09585192.2016.1244699]

Marler, J.H., Boudreau, J.W. (2020). A comprehensive examination of the effects of human resource management practises on business performance. *Manage. Rev., 46*(6), 1156-1186.

Rasmussen, T., Ulrich, D. (2020). Practise makes perfect. How HR analytics avoids becoming a management style. *Organ. Dyn., 49*(3).
[http://dx.doi.org/10.1016/j.orgdyn.2015.05.008]

Rasmussen, T., Ulrich, D. (2015). Learning from practice: how HR analytics avoids being a management fad. *Organ. Dyn., 44*(3), 236-242.
[http://dx.doi.org/10.1016/j.orgdyn.2015.05.008]

Sumathi Annamalai, Muralidhar Deshpande *et al* (2015). Exploring current practices and future trends in HR Analytics among VUCA Organizations: A Study. HR Summit & International Conference at IIM, Raipur August 21-22, 2015.

Van den Heuvel, S., Bondarouk, T., Strohmeier, S. (2020). How can analytics impact human resource management? The role of logical HRM systems, logical maturity, and HRM impact. *Int. J. Hum. Resour. Manage., 31*(18), 2397-2426.

CHAPTER 5

Unleashing the Power of HR Analytics: Enhancing People Management Strategies

Parulkumari Bhati[1,*]

[1] *Department of Humanities and Social Science, Institute of Technology, Nirma University, Gujarat, India*

Abstract: HR analytics can enable organizations to make data-driven decisions that improve workforce productivity, engagement, and retention. This chapter provides an overview of the key HR analytics concepts and methods, including data collection and analysis, data visualization, and predictive modeling. It also focuses on the challenges and opportunities associated with implementing HR analytics in organizations, such as data privacy and security concerns and the need for skilled data analysts. Overall, the article makes a case for HR analytics as a critical tool for driving organizational success in the modern workplace. The use of HR analytics has become increasingly important in enhancing people management strategies. This chapter also explores the potential of HR analytics to transform the way organizations manage their workforce, from recruitment to retention. By leveraging data and analytics, HR experts can gain an understanding of their workforce, identify areas for improvement, and make data-driven decisions. This chapter discusses the benefits of HR analytics, including improved talent acquisition, enhanced employee engagement and retention, and increased productivity. It also examines some of the challenges organizations may face when implementing HR analytics, such as data privacy concerns and the need for specialized skills. Overall, this chapter demonstrates how HR analytics can be a powerful device for establishments looking to augment their people management policies.

Keywords: Data-driven decision-making, Employee engagement, HR analytics, Performance management, People management, Organizational effectiveness, Retention, Talent acquisition, Workforce planning.

INTRODUCTION TO HR ANALYTICS AND ITS SIGNIFICANCE IN MODERN BUSINESS

In today's quickly growing business landscape, where data is often dubbed the "new oil", the field of human resources (HR) has undergone a profound trans-

---

* **Corresponding author Parulkumari Bhati:** Department of Humanities and Social Science, Institute of Technology, Nirma University, Gujarat, India; E-mail: dr.parulbhati@gmail.com

Sandeep Kumar Kautish & Anuj Sheopuri (Eds.)

formation. Traditional HR practices, while effective in their time, are being superseded by a new approach that is revolutionizing the way organizations manage their most valuable asset: their people. This transformation is none other than the rise of HR analytics.

Defining HR Analytics

HR analytics, identified as people analytics or personnel analytics, involves the systematic collection, analysis, and interpretation of HR-related data to drive evidence-based decisions and strategies. It is the marriage of data science and human resources, harnessing the power of data to unravel insights that enable organizations to make informed and proactive people management decisions.

The Power of Data-Driven Insights

In an era where digital technologies permeate every aspect of business, HR analytics emerges as a game-changer. It is not merely about digitizing old HR processes; it is about unlocking the latent potential within workforce data to inform strategic actions. HR analytics takes HR from a reactive support function to a proactive driver of organizational success.

The Significance in Modern Business

The significance of HR analytics in modern business is multifaceted. Here are some key aspects highlighting its importance.

Informed Decision-Making

HR analytics equips HR professionals and organizational leaders with insights that go beyond gut feelings. Decisions are no longer based solely on intuition; they are anchored in empirical evidence derived from data analysis.

Enhanced Recruitment

In a globalized talent market, finding the right candidates swiftly is crucial. HR analytics optimizes recruitment processes by identifying the most effective sourcing channels, predicting candidate success, and ensuring cultural fit.

Employee Retention and Engagement

High turnover rates can be detrimental to a company's bottom line. HR analytics identifies underlying factors contributing to turnover, allowing organizations to implement targeted strategies for improving employee satisfaction and retention.

Performance Optimization

By analyzing performance metrics and team dynamics, HR analytics helps identify factors that contribute to high-performing teams. Insights guide decisions on team composition, leadership styles, and skill development.

Strategic Workforce Planning

With the future of work evolving, organizations need to anticipate skill gaps and workforce needs. HR analytics enables proactive workforce planning by forecasting talent demands and supply.

Personalized Learning and Development

Employees today seek continuous growth. HR analytics tailors learning and development paths based on individual skills, preferences, and career aspirations, fostering a culture of learning.

Ethical and Inclusive Practices

HR analytics has the potential to uncover biases and disparities within organizations. By identifying these issues, companies can work toward building a more equitable and inclusive workforce.

In essence, HR analytics transcends traditional HR functions and positions HR as a strategic partner in achieving organizational goals. It aligns HR initiatives with business objectives, enhances employee experiences, and maximizes overall performance.

As we journey through this chapter, we will delve deeper into the applications, benefits, challenges, and future trends of HR analytics, exploring how it revolutionizes people management strategies and empowers organizations to make smarter, data-driven decisions.

The Transformation from Traditional HR Practices to Data-Driven Decision-Making

The evolution of human resources (HR) practices from manual, intuition-based processes to data-driven decision-making represents a profound shift in how organizations manage their workforce. This transformation is reshaping the HR landscape and revolutionizing the way businesses approach people management. Let's explore the key milestones in this journey and the advantages that data-driven HR decision-making brings to the table.

From Paper to Pixels: Digitalization of HR Records

Traditional HR practices often involve mountains of paperwork, making record-keeping and retrieval a time-consuming endeavor. The advent of digital technology led to the creation of HR Information Systems (HRIS), enabling organizations to store and manage employee data electronically. This marked the initial step toward centralization and accessibility of HR data.

The Emergence of HR Metrics and Reporting

As technology advanced, HR began to incorporate basic metrics and reporting into their practices. These early data points included headcount, turnover rates, and time-to-fill for job vacancies. However, the focus remained on descriptive analytics, providing historical insights without necessarily informing future strategies.

Transition to Predictive Analytics

With the growth of computing power and data analysis tools, HR moved into the realm of predictive analytics. By analyzing historical data, organizations could anticipate trends and outcomes. For example, predictive analytics allowed HR teams to foresee potential talent gaps and make informed decisions about recruitment and training initiatives.

From Intuition to Evidence-Based Insights

The transition from relying solely on HR professionals' intuition to embracing evidence-based insights was a watershed moment. Data-driven decision-making armed HR professionals with objective information to support their strategies. Instead of making assumptions about employee preferences or engagement drivers, they could rely on data-backed conclusions.

Enhanced Recruitment Strategies

Traditionally, recruitment often relied on job descriptions and resumes. The introduction of data analytics revolutionized this process. HR teams could now analyze the success rate of candidates from different sources, identify patterns in successful hires, and refine recruitment strategies accordingly. This shift improved the accuracy of candidate selection and cultural fit.

Tailored Learning and Development

Data-driven insights enable HR to personalize learning and development paths for employees. By analyzing skill gaps, career aspirations, and learning preferences, organizations can offer training that aligns with individual growth trajectories. This tailored approach enhances employee engagement and skill development.

Proactive Employee Retention

Predictive analytics also play a pivotal role in employee retention. By analyzing factors contributing to turnover—such as job satisfaction, compensation, and work-life balance—HR teams can intervene before employees decide to leave. Proactive strategies, informed by data, can significantly reduce turnover rates.

Strategic Workforce Planning

Data-driven decision-making extends to strategic workforce planning. Organizations can anticipate future skill requirements based on industry trends, technological advancements, and business goals. This proactive approach ensures that the right talent is available when needed.

Ethical and Inclusive Practices

Data-driven HR practices help identify unconscious biases and disparities within organizations. By analyzing data related to promotions, pay equity, and representation, HR can address inequities and promote diversity and inclusion.

In conclusion, the transformation from traditional HR practices to data-driven decision-making has revolutionized people management strategies. The integration of advanced analytics allows HR to move beyond reactive measures and become proactive contributors to organizational success. The journey continues as emerging technologies like artificial intelligence and machine learning further elevate the role of HR in shaping the future of work.

Enhancing People Management Strategies through HR Analytics

In an era of data abundance, human resources (HR) has evolved from administrative support to a strategic powerhouse. The integration of HR analytics has been instrumental in this evolution, fundamentally changing how organizations approach people management. Here, we delve into how HR analytics enhances people management strategies, yielding benefits across various aspects of the employee lifecycle.

Informed Recruitment and Selection

HR analytics transforms recruitment from a subjective process to an objective science. By analyzing historical hiring data, organizations can identify the most effective sourcing channels, ensuring that they invest resources where they yield the best results. Moreover, predictive analytics can assess the likelihood of a candidate's success based on their attributes and competencies, leading to more accurate selection decisions.

Precise Employee Onboarding

Data-driven insights enable HR to customize the onboarding experience for new employees. By analyzing past onboarding outcomes, organizations can refine the process to ensure that new hires quickly acclimate to their roles and the company culture, setting the stage for long-term engagement.

Employee Engagement and Retention

HR analytics empowers organizations to dive deep into factors influencing employee engagement and retention. Surveys and performance metrics can be analyzed to uncover correlations between engagement drivers and organizational outcomes. With this information, HR can implement targeted strategies to enhance employee satisfaction, ultimately reducing turnover rates.

Personalized Learning and Development

One-size-fits-all training is a thing of the past. HR analytics enables the design of personalized learning paths based on individual skills, career aspirations, and learning preferences. This not only enhances employee development but also aligns with the organization's strategic goals.

Optimized Performance Management

Performance evaluations become more meaningful with HR analytics. Objective data, rather than subjective impressions, forms the basis of evaluations. This eliminates biases and allows for fairer, more accurate assessments, fostering a culture of meritocracy.

Effective Team Composition

Understanding what makes high-performing teams tick is critical. HR analytics analyzes team dynamics, collaboration patterns, and performance outcomes to identify the traits and behaviors that lead to success. Organizations can then replicate these dynamics across different teams.

Proactive Succession Planning

By analyzing employee skills, competencies, and career trajectories, HR analytics supports succession planning. Organizations can identify potential future leaders and groom them for leadership roles, ensuring a smooth transition when key personnel move on.

Workforce Diversity and Inclusion

HR analytics plays a pivotal role in promoting diversity and inclusion. Data analysis can identify areas where representation falls short and provide insights into the factors contributing to disparities. Armed with this knowledge, HR can implement targeted initiatives to create a more diverse and inclusive workforce.

Strategic Workforce Planning

Anticipating the future workforce landscape is essential. HR analytics forecasts skill demands and supply, enabling organizations to prepare for evolving industry trends and technological shifts. This proactive approach ensures the availability of the right talent when needed.

In a nutshell, HR analytics is a catalyst for aligning people management strategies with business objectives. By replacing guesswork with data-backed insights, organizations can enhance employee experiences, optimize performance, and foster a culture of continuous improvement. As the field of HR analytics continues to evolve, its potential to reshape the workplace is only beginning to be realized.

UNDERSTANDING HR ANALYTICS

HR analytics refers to the process of assembling, evaluating, and considering data related to human resources and workforce dynamics to make informed decisions that drive organizational success. Unlike traditional HR practices that often rely on intuition and experience, HR analytics is driven by insights derived from data.

Data sources for HR analytics are diverse, encompassing employee records, performance metrics, training and development outcomes, recruitment data, employee surveys, and even external data like market trends and demographic shifts. These data points, when processed through advanced analytical tools and techniques, unveil patterns, correlations, and trends that can guide strategic HR initiatives.

HR analytics, also recognized as labor force analytics or people analytics, refers to the systematic use of data, statistical analysis, and data-driven insights to inform and improve various aspects of human resources management. It involves the application of data science techniques to HR data in order to gain deeper insights into workforce trends, behaviors, and outcomes, ultimately guiding strategic decision-making within organizations.

Core Components of HR Analytics

Data Collection and Integration

HR analytics begins with the collection of relevant data from various sources within the organization. This data can include employee records, performance evaluations, training records, recruitment data, compensation information, and more. Data integration involves centralizing data from disparate sources into a unified database for analysis.

Data Cleaning and Preprocessing

Raw data often contain errors, inconsistencies, and missing values. Data cleaning involves the process of identifying and rectifying these issues to ensure the accuracy and reliability of the data. Pre-processing steps might include removing duplicate entries, filling in missing values, and standardizing data formats.

Descriptive Analytics

Descriptive analytics focuses on summarizing historical data to provide insights into past trends and occurrences. It includes metrics such as headcount, turnover rates, average employee tenure, and diversity ratios. Descriptive analytics forms the foundation upon which more advanced analytics are built.

Diagnostic Analytics

Diagnostic analytics delves deeper into the "why" behind the descriptive metrics. It involves analyzing patterns and relationships within the data to identify the factors influencing workforce trends. For instance, diagnostic analytics could explore why certain teams have higher turnover rates than others, uncovering potential contributing factors.

Predictive Analytics

Predictive analytics in HR analytics is akin to peering through a crystal ball made of data. Its capacity to extrapolate future possibilities from historical information fuels proactive decision-making, resource optimization, and talent nurturing, ultimately setting the stage for a future-ready workforce.

Prescriptive Analytics

Prescriptive analytics prescriptive goes beyond prediction, offering actionable recommendations derived from data analysis. This advanced approach not only anticipates potential outcomes but also guides stakeholders on the precise steps needed to attain desired results. As an illustration, in the context of reducing turnover, prescriptive analytics could propose targeted strategies grounded in predictive models to curtail attrition rates.

Data Visualization and Reporting

Communicating complex data insights effectively is crucial. Data visualization tools and dashboards transform intricate HR data into visual representations, making it easier for HR professionals and organizational leaders to grasp trends and patterns at a glance.

Ethical Considerations

An essential component of HR analytics is the ethical handling of employee data. Ensuring data privacy, security, and compliance with relevant regulations is paramount. Ethical considerations involve obtaining informed consent, anonymizing data when necessary, and protecting sensitive information.

Continuous Improvement

HR analytics is an iterative process. As organizations collect more data and gain insights, they can refine their analytical models, strategies, and decision-making processes. Continuous improvement involves learning from previous analyses and adapting to changing workforce dynamics.

In essence, HR analytics empowers HR professionals and organizational leaders to make evidence-based decisions by transforming raw data into actionable insights. By leveraging the core components of HR analytics, organizations can enhance workforce management, improve employee experiences, and contribute to the overall success of the business.

The Process to Collect - HR-Related Data

HR analytics involves a systematic approach to collecting, analyzing, and rendering HR-related data to derive meaningful understandings that inform strategic supervisory. This process requires careful planning, data management, statistical analysis, and thoughtful interpretation. Here's a breakdown of each step in the process:

Data Collection

The first step is to obtain related data from various sources within the organization. These sources may include:

Employee Records

Personal information, job roles, tenure, and performance history.

Recruitment Data

Application sources, hiring timelines, and candidate profiles.

Training and Development Records

Training courses, completion rates, and skills acquired.

Compensation and Benefits Data

Salary structures, bonuses, and benefits information.

Performance Metrics

Key performance indicators (KPIs), performance evaluations, and productivity metrics.

Employee Surveys

Engagement surveys, feedback, and satisfaction ratings.

External Data

Market trends, industry benchmarks, and demographic data.

Data Preparation and Cleaning

Raw data often require cleaning and preparation before analysis. This involves:

Data Validation

Ensuring data correctness and consistency, identifying and correcting errors or inconsistencies.

Handling Missing Values

Dealing with data fields that have missing values through imputation or other methods.

Data Transformation

Converting data into a standardized format for analysis.

Removing Duplicates

Eliminating duplicated entries to avoid skewing results.

Data Analysis

After data preparation, various analytical techniques are applied to extract insights:

Descriptive Analysis

Summarizing data using statistics and visualizations to understand historical trends, distributions, and patterns.

Diagnostic Analysis

Investigating relationships between variables to identify causes of specific HR outcomes.

Predictive Analysis

Developing models to predict future trends or outcomes based on historical data.

Prescriptive Analysis

Recommending actions based on predictive models and simulation scenarios.

Interpretation of Insights

Interpreting insights involves understanding what the data reveals and extracting actionable information:

Contextual Understanding

Put insights into the context of the organization's goals, industry trends, and business strategies.

Identifying Patterns

Recognize trends, correlations, and anomalies in the data that might impact HR decisions.

Strategic Implications

Determine how the insights align with HR and organizational goals, and identify potential areas for improvement.

Decision-Making

Translate insights into actionable strategies that enhance workforce management, employee engagement, and organizational performance.

Communication

The final step is to effectively communicate the findings and recommendations:

Data Visualization

Present insights using graphs, charts, and dashboards that convey information clearly and intuitively.

Narrative Explanation

Provide a narrative that explains the significance of the insights and their implications for HR and the organization.

Stakeholder Engagement

Share insights with relevant stakeholders, such as HR teams, management, and executives.

Actionable Recommendations

Offer concrete recommendations based on the analysis that can drive strategic HR decisions.

Continuous Improvement

HR analytics is an ongoing process. As new data is collected and insights are gained, organizations should continuously refine their analytical methods and strategies to align with changing workforce dynamics and organizational goals.

In essence, the process of collecting, analyzing, and interpreting HR-related data is a structured approach that empowers organizations to make informed and data-driven decisions to optimize people management strategies and enhance overall organizational performance.

THE ROLE OF DATA-DRIVEN INSIGHTS IN STRATEGIC DECISION-MAKING

In an era where information is abundant, the ability to make informed decisions is a critical differentiator for organizations. Data-driven insights have emerged as a powerful tool, transforming the way strategic decisions are made across various facets of business. Within this landscape, the role of data-driven insights in strategic decision-making takes center stage, revolutionizing how organizations formulate, evaluate, and execute their strategies. Nowhere is this impact more evident than in human resources (HR), where workforce dynamics and employee engagement heavily influence an organization's success. Here's a deep dive into the pivotal role of data-driven insights in strategic decision-making within HR

Informed Decision-Making

Data-driven insights provide a solid foundation for decision-making. Instead of relying on gut feelings or intuition, HR professionals can draw on concrete data to support their choices. Whether it is optimizing recruitment processes, refining compensation strategies, or developing targeted employee engagement initiatives, decisions rooted in data are more likely to yield positive outcomes.

Evidence-Based Strategy Formulation

Strategic decision-making involves formulating strategies that align with long-term organizational goals. Data-driven insights serve as evidence that supports the viability of these strategies. For instance, when devising a talent development strategy, insights derived from analyzing historical performance data can indicate which training programs yield the best results, enabling HR to design effective learning paths.

Mitigating Risk

Every decision carries an element of risk. Data-driven insights help mitigate risks by providing a comprehensive view of potential outcomes. In HR, predictive analytics can anticipate turnover risks, allowing organizations to proactively implement measures to retain key talent. By identifying and addressing these risks early, organizations can avoid costly disruptions.

Objective Evaluation

Data-driven insights foster objectivity in evaluating alternative strategies. In HR, this is particularly significant when assessing performance metrics or compensation structures. Objectivity ensures fairness and consistency, reducing the potential for biases that might impact decision-making.

Measurable Impact

Strategic decisions should be measurable in terms of their impact. Data-driven insights facilitate the tracking of key performance indicators (KPIs) and metrics.

For instance, when implementing employee engagement initiatives, organizations can track changes in engagement scores over time, gauging the success of their strategies.

Flexibility and Agility

The business landscape is dynamic, requiring organizations to adapt swiftly to changing circumstances. Data-driven insights empower HR to monitor trends and respond promptly. Whether adjusting recruitment strategies due to shifts in talent demand or realigning learning and development programs based on emerging skill requirements, data-driven insights enhance organizational agility.

Alignment with Organizational Goals

Strategic decisions must align with overarching organizational objectives. Data-driven insights provide the compass for this alignment. By analyzing the impact of HR initiatives on bottom-line metrics, such as revenue, profit, or customer satisfaction, organizations can ensure that HR strategies contribute directly to business success.

Enhancing Employee Experience

At the heart of HR lies the goal of optimizing the employee experience. Data-driven insights enable HR to tailor initiatives to individual needs, preferences, and aspirations. By analyzing engagement survey data or performance metrics, organizations can pinpoint areas where employee experiences can be enhanced, resulting in higher job satisfaction and retention rates.

In conclusion, the role of data-driven insights in strategic decision-making within HR is transformative. It elevates HR from a transactional function to a strategic partner that influences the course of the organization. By leveraging data to inform decisions, organizations enhance their ability to make choices that optimize workforce management, improve employee engagement, and ultimately contribute to their competitive advantage in the marketplace.

BENEFITS OF HR ANALYTICS FOR PEOPLE MANAGEMENT

HR analytics, the practice of using data-driven insights to enhance human resources management, has emerged as a cornerstone of modern organizational success. By leveraging data to inform people management strategies, businesses can unlock a multitude of benefits that span the entire employee lifecycle. Here are some of the key advantages HR analytics brings to people management:

Informed Decision-Making

HR analytics provides decision-makers with objective, data-backed insights. This empowers HR professionals and organizational leaders to make informed choices that align with business goals rather than relying on gut feelings or intuition.

Enhanced Recruitment Strategies

Data-driven insights optimize recruitment processes. Organizations can identify the most effective sourcing channels, tailor job descriptions to attract suitable candidates and predict candidate success based on historical data. This results in quicker and more accurate hiring decisions.

Improved Employee Retention

By analyzing factors contributing to turnover, HR analytics helps organizations proactively identify attrition risks and implement targeted retention strategies. This leads to improved job satisfaction, reduced turnover rates, and better organizational stability.

Personalized Learning and Development

HR analytics tailors learning and development programs to individual employee needs. By analyzing performance data and skill gaps, organizations can offer training that aligns with employee aspirations, fostering continuous learning and skill enhancement.

Performance Optimization

Insights derived from HR analytics inform performance management strategies. Organizations can identify top performers, uncover areas for improvement, and develop actionable plans to enhance overall workforce productivity and effectiveness.

Strategic Workforce Planning

HR analytics enables organizations to forecast future skill demands and workforce needs based on industry trends and business goals. This proactive approach ensures the availability of the right talent when required, preventing skill gaps.

Employee Engagement Enhancement

Engagement surveys and feedback data become more impactful when analyzed using HR analytics. Organizations can identify drivers of engagement, address pain points, and design initiatives that improve overall employee satisfaction and morale.

Objective Diversity and Inclusion Initiatives

HR analytics helps organizations identify disparities and biases within the workforce. By analyzing data related to diversity metrics and representation, HR can develop targeted strategies to promote a more inclusive workplace.

Effective Succession Planning

HR analytics aids in identifying high-potential employees and developing tailored succession plans. Organizations can groom the next generation of leaders and ensure a smooth transition when key personnel move on.

Measurable Return on Investment (ROI)

HR analytics quantifies the impact of HR initiatives on key business metrics. This enables HR professionals to demonstrate the ROI of their strategies, making a compelling case for the value they bring to the organization.

Data-Driven Culture

Adopting HR analytics cultivates a data-driven culture within the organization. When employees see decisions being made based on evidence rather than assumptions, they are more likely to embrace data-driven practices in their own roles.

Continuous Improvement

HR analytics is a continuous process. As organizations collect more data and gain insights, they can refine their strategies and adapt to changing workforce dynamics, fostering a culture of continuous improvement.

In essence, the benefits of HR analytics for people management are far-reaching. By harnessing the power of data, organizations can optimize HR practices, engage employees more effectively, and drive overall organizational success.

APPLICATION OF HR ANALYTICS IN PEOPLE MANAGEMENT

HR analytics is revolutionizing the way organizations manage their workforce by providing data-driven insights that inform strategic decision-making. Its applications span every stage of the employee lifecycle, enabling HR professionals to optimize processes, enhance engagement, and align strategies with business goals. Here are some key applications of HR analytics in people management:

Recruitment and Talent Acquisition

Sourcing Optimization

Analyze historical recruitment data to identify the most effective sourcing channels for candidates.

Candidate Success Prediction

Utilize predictive analytics to assess candidate success based on attributes, skills, and competencies.

Cultural Fit Assessment

Analyze data to ensure candidates align with the company culture, enhancing retention rates.

Employee Onboarding and Integration

Onboarding Effectiveness

Evaluate the success of onboarding programs by analyzing the performance metrics of newly onboarded employees.

Time to Productivity

Track the time it takes for new hires to become fully productive, identifying areas for improvement.

Performance Management

Objective Performance Evaluations

Use data to ensure fair and unbiased performance evaluations, reducing subjectivity and bias.

Performance Trends

Analyze performance data over time to identify patterns, strengths, and areas for development.

Learning and Development

Skill Gap Identification

Analyze performance and training data to identify skill gaps and tailor learning programs.

Learning Impact

Measure the impact of training on employee performance and business outcomes.

Employee Engagement and Retention

Engagement Insights

Analyze survey data and feedback to identify drivers of engagement and design targeted initiatives.

Attrition Risk Prediction

Use predictive analytics to identify employees at risk of leaving, allowing for proactive intervention.

Team Dynamics and Collaboration

Team Composition

Analyze team composition and performance to identify optimal team structures and dynamics.

Collaboration Patterns

Use data to understand how teams collaborate and share knowledge, enhancing cross-functional cooperation.

Compensation and Benefits

Fair Compensation

Analyze compensation data to ensure pay equity and identify any disparities.

Benefit Preferences

Use data to understand employee preferences for benefits and tailor offerings accordingly.

Succession Planning

High-Potential Identification

Analyze performance and competency data to identify high-potential employees for leadership roles.

Leadership Development

Design succession plans and development programs based on data-driven insights.

Diversity and Inclusion

Representation Analysis

Analyze demographic data to assess representation across various groups and identify gaps.

Inclusion Initiatives

Develop targeted strategies to foster an inclusive workplace based on insights derived from data.

Exit and Turnover Analysis

Turnover Causes

Analyze exit interview data to identify reasons for turnover and develop strategies to address them.

Cost of Turnover

Calculate the financial impact of turnover to justify retention strategies.

Workforce Planning

Future Skill Demands

Analyze industry trends and business forecasts to predict future skill requirements.

Talent Supply Forecasting

Use data to predict the availability of talent in the market for strategic workforce planning.

Incorporating HR analytics into people management strategies enables organizations to make evidence-based decisions, enhance employee experiences, and drive organizational success. By leveraging data-driven insights, HR professionals can optimize processes, foster a culture of continuous improvement, and ensure that their strategies align with both employee needs and business objectives.

ETHICAL CONSIDERATIONS IN HR ANALYTICS

While HR analytics offers numerous benefits for people management, it also raises important ethical considerations that organizations must address to ensure responsible and fair use of employee data. As data-driven decision-making becomes integral to HR practices, it is essential to uphold ethical standards and protect the rights and privacy of individuals. Here are some key ethical considerations in HR analytics:

Data Privacy and Consent

Informed Consent & Data Security

In the dynamic landscape of analytics, data privacy and consent form the ethical foundation on which organizations build their strategies. By respecting individuals' rights and making ethical choices, organizations can harness the power of data while upholding the trust and confidence of those whose information they rely upon.

Transparency

Clear Communication

Provide employees with transparent information about how their data will be used for analytics. Transparency builds trust and ensures that employees are aware of the purposes and implications of data analysis.

Fairness and Non-Discrimination

Avoiding Bias

Ensure that data analysis and models are designed to be unbiased and do not discriminate against any particular group. Biased algorithms can perpetuate inequalities and negatively impact underrepresented groups.

Equal Treatment

Ensure that analytics-based decisions, such as promotions, compensation, and training opportunities, are applied fairly and consistently across all employees.

Anonymization and De-Identification

Protecting Privacy

Anonymize or de-identify data whenever possible to prevent the identification of individuals. This minimizes the risk of exposing personal information while still allowing for meaningful analysis.

Accountability and Ownership

Ownership of Data

Clearly define who owns the data collected and analyzed. This is especially important when collaborating with third-party analytics providers.

Accountability

Establish clear lines of accountability for data handling, analysis, and decision-making. This ensures that responsible parties are held accountable for the ethical use of HR analytics.

Use Limitations

Scope of Use

Clearly define the intended scope of using HR analytics insights. Avoid using data for purposes beyond what employees have consented to or what is ethically appropriate.

Employee Empowerment

Access to Data

Allow employees to access their own data and insights generated through analytics. This empowers employees to understand how their data is being used and make informed decisions.

Continuous Monitoring and Auditing

Ethical Review

Establish regular monitoring and auditing processes to ensure that HR analytics practices adhere to ethical guidelines and regulations.

Adjustments

If ethical concerns or unintended consequences arise, organizations should be prepared to adjust their analytics practices accordingly.

Cultural and Social Sensitivity

Respecting Diversity

Ensure that HR analytics takes into account cultural and social differences that might impact data interpretation and decision-making.

Compliance with Regulations

Legal Frameworks

Understand and comply with data protection and privacy regulations applicable in your jurisdiction, such as the General Data Protection Regulation (GDPR) in the European Union or the Health Insurance Portability and Accountability Act (HIPAA) in the United States.

Incorporating these ethical considerations into HR analytics practices not only safeguards employee rights and privacy but also enhances the credibility of data-driven decision-making. Organizations that prioritize ethics in HR analytics build a foundation of trust with their employees and stakeholders while maximizing the benefits of data insights for people management.

CHALLENGES AND FUTURE TRENDS

HR analytics has the potential to revolutionize people management, but it also comes with its fair share of challenges and exciting future trends. As organizations continue to embrace data-driven approaches to HR, they must navigate these challenges while keeping an eye on emerging trends that can reshape the landscape. Here are some of the key challenges and future trends in HR analytics:

Challenges

Data Quality and Integration

Challenge

Confirming data accuracy, uniformity, and mixing from various sources can be multifaceted and time-consuming.

Impact

Poor data quality can lead to inaccurate insights and compromised decision-making.

Data Privacy and Ethics

Challenge

Balancing the need for data-driven insights with ethical considerations and data privacy regulations.

Impact

Mishandling employee data can erode trust and lead to legal and reputational risks.

Skill Gap and Talent Shortage

Challenge

A shortage of skilled HR analytics professionals who can analyze and interpret data effectively.

Impact

The lack of expertise can hinder an organization's ability to leverage analytics for strategic decision-making.

Resistance to Change

Challenge

Employees and HR professionals may resist the shift to data-driven practices due to a fear of job displacement or skepticism about the effectiveness of analytics.

Bias and Fairness

Challenge

Unconscious biases can be encoded in algorithms and models, perpetuating biases in hiring, performance evaluations, and other HR processes.

Technology and Infrastructure

Challenge

Implementing the necessary technology infrastructure for data collection, storage, analysis, and visualization can be resource-intensive.

Future Trends

Predictive and Prescriptive Analytics

Trend

The evolution from descriptive analytics to predictive and prescriptive analytics, where HR professionals not only understand historical trends but also predict future outcomes and recommend actions to optimize them.

AI and Machine Learning

Trend

Increasing use of artificial intelligence and machine learning algorithms to process and analyze vast amounts of data, uncover patterns, and make data-driven predictions.

Employee Experience Analytics

Trend

A focus on using analytics to enhance employee experiences, including personalized learning paths, career development plans, and real-time feedback mechanisms.

Workforce Planning for Remote and Hybrid Work

Trend

With the rise of remote and hybrid work, HR analytics will play a pivotal role in forecasting talent needs and optimizing workforce distribution.

Emotional and Sentiment Analysis

Trend

Leveraging advanced analytics to gauge employee emotions and sentiments through textual analysis of surveys, emails, and social media.

Real-Time Analytics

Trend

The move towards real-time analytics that allow organizations to respond to workforce trends and issues promptly.

Natural Language Processing (NLP)

Trend

Using NLP to analyze written and spoken communication to gain insights into employee sentiments, engagement, and concerns.

Integration with HR Technology

Trend

HR analytics will increasingly integrate with HR technology systems, providing seamless access to data and insights within existing workflows.

Ethical AI and Responsible Analytics

Trend

A focus on developing AI systems and analytics practices that are ethical, transparent, and free from biases.

Skill Development for HR Analytics

Trend

The growth of training programs and educational resources to address the skill gap in HR analytics and data interpretation.

As organizations adapt to these challenges and embrace these trends, HR analytics will continue to evolve, transforming the role of HR from transactional processes to strategic partners in shaping the workforce and organizational success.

CONCLUSION

Unleashing the power of HR analytics empowers organizations to optimize their people management strategies. By leveraging data-driven insights, HR professionals can make informed decisions that drive employee engagement, improve performance, and align HR initiatives with organizational goals. However, the journey towards effective HR analytics implementation requires a combination of technological investment, analytical skills, and ethical considerations. As the digital era continues to reshape the business landscape, embracing HR analytics will be a pivotal step in shaping the future of people management.

In the ever-evolving landscape of modern business, the integration of HR analytics has emerged as a driving force behind innovative and effective people management strategies. From traditional HR practices to data-driven decision-making, organizations have embarked on a transformative journey that empowers them to harness the full potential of their workforce. The journey from intuition to evidence, from reactive to proactive, has revolutionized how businesses approach human resources management.

The journey begins with understanding the core components of HR analytics – the collection, analysis, and interpretation of data. This process enables organizations to uncover insights that are essential for strategic decision-making across the employee lifecycle. The power of data-driven insights is evident in how they inform recruitment, optimize onboarding, enhance employee engagement, refine performance management, and guide succession planning. Ethical considerations underpin these efforts, ensuring that employee data is handled responsibly, transparently, and in compliance with regulations.

The benefits of HR analytics are far-reaching. Organizations gain a competitive edge by making informed decisions, aligning strategies with business objectives, and nurturing a data-driven culture. Recruitment becomes more targeted, retention strategies are proactive, and employee development is personalized. Teams collaborate effectively, diversity is promoted, and the employee experience is elevated. As HR analytics becomes more sophisticated, its impact on organizational success becomes increasingly profound.

However, challenges abound, from data quality and privacy concerns to the need for specialized skills and managing biases. Yet, these challenges are opportunities for growth, pushing organizations to adopt ethical practices, invest in skill development, and create a foundation of trust with employees.

Looking ahead, the future of HR analytics is exciting and transformative. The evolution from descriptive to predictive and prescriptive analytics promises to deliver even deeper insights. AI, machine learning, and real-time analytics will reshape how organizations understand and manage their workforce. Ethical considerations will be paramount in developing responsible AI and analytics practices.

In conclusion, the power of HR analytics lies in its ability to unlock the potential of people, transforming them from mere employees to strategic assets. By combining data-driven insights with ethical practices, organizations can create a workplace that nurtures talent, drives innovation, and propels them toward sustainable success in a rapidly changing world. The journey continues as HR analytics evolves, and organizations continue to unleash its transformative power for enhanced people management strategies.

REFERENCES

Bondarouk, T.V., Ruël, H.J.M. (2009). Electronic Human Resource Management: challenges in the digital era. *Int. J. Hum. Resour. Manage., 20*(3), 505-514.
[http://dx.doi.org/10.1080/09585190802707235]

Boudreau, J. W., & Cascio, W. F. (2017). Investing in People: Financial Impact of Human Resource Initiatives. FT Press.

Becker, B., Gerhart, B. (1996). The impact of human resource management on organizational performance: Progress and prospects. *Acad. Manage. J., 39*(4), 779-801.
[http://dx.doi.org/10.2307/256712]

Colakoglu, S., Culha, O. (2010). HR analytics: A systematic literature review. *Int. J. Inf. Manage., 30*(5), 416-423.

Davenport, T.H. (2018). Data scientist: The sexiest job of the 21st century. *Harv. Bus. Rev.*

[PMID: 23074866]

Fitz-enz, J. (1995). How to Measure Human Resource Management. McGraw-Hill.

Huselid, M.A. (1995). The impact of human resource management practices on turnover, productivity, and corporate financial performance. *Acad. Manage. J., 38*(3), 635-672. [http://dx.doi.org/10.2307/256741]

Lawler III, E. E. (2018). Agile Talent: How to Source and Manage Outside Experts. Harvard Business Review Press.

Rasmussen, H.S., Ulrich, D. (2015). Learning to Learn: The Pathway to Learning Agility. *RBL Group.*

Redman, T.C. (2015). The problem with HR analytics. Harvard Business Review.

CHAPTER 6

Predicting Employee Performance Using Predictive Models

Sasirekha V.[1,*], **Gomuprakash P.**[2] and **Suresh R.**[3]

[1] *Faculty of Management, SRM Institute of Science & Technology, Vadapalani, Chennai, India*

[2] *Sri Sairam Engineering College, Chennai, India*

[3] *Management Studies, Sri Sairam Engineering College, Chennai, India*

Abstract: An employee performance forecasting overview typically outlines the key components and objectives of a forecasting model developed to assess employee effectiveness in the workplace. Such models include employee demographics, job-related factors (job description, tenure, *etc.*), performance metrics (sales figures, customer feedback, *etc.*), and psychometric scores (personality traits, cognitive abilities). The goal of such models is to identify the factors most strongly associated with high performance and use this information to predict future employee success. This chapter describes potential challenges and limitations associated with the predictive models, such as ethical concerns about the use of personal data, the potential for bias or error in predictive algorithms, and the need to balance the benefits of predictive modeling with concerns about employee privacy and autonomy.

Keywords: Employee performance, Ethical concerns, Predictive models.

INTRODUCTION

In the fast-paced and ruthless world of modern business, corporations are acutely aware that their workforce is their most significant and valuable asset (Fulmer, Ingrid & Ployhart, Robert, 2013). This is because labor is one of the primary factors that determine a company's profitability. The success and growth of every company are closely related to the productivity of its employees (Olaniyi, Olusegun Abayomi, 2021). As a result of this, businesses are always on the lookout for novel and original approaches that will allow them to boost the productivity, engagement, and overall performance of their staff. It has become a crucial component in this effort to attempt to predict how personnel will carry out

[*] **Corresponding author Sasirekha V.:** Faculty of Management, SRM Institute of Science & Technology, Vadapalani, Chennai, India; E-mail: prof.sasirekha@gmail.com

their duties. Using the strength of modern data analytics and predictive modeling, a corporation may get insights about its employees' potential, work patterns, and future contributions. This predictive strategy assists businesses in making well-informed decisions, effectively allocating resources, and effectively designing strategies to increase both individual and team performance (Cascio, W. F., 2006). In this age of digital transition, the traditional approaches to management and performance evaluation have been proven to be insufficient and backward-looking. This is because they focus on the past rather than looking toward the future. In the modern world of business, firms are shifting more toward proactive and data-driven initiatives in order to gain a deeper understanding of the factors that impact employee performance (Chowdhury S, Hioe E, and Schaninger B, 2018). By drawing on a wide range of different data sources, businesses are able to develop predictive models that provide an all-encompassing view of their workforce. These data sources might include things like employee feedback and external market trends, in addition to historical performance metrics and results from projects. This study will center on researching the topic of predictive analytics as it pertains to employee performance as its primary objective. During this discussion, we will study how new methods and cutting-edge technology are reshaping the manner in which corporations identify high-potential workers, reduce performance bottlenecks, and encourage ongoing progress. If companies can harness the power of machine learning, artificial intelligence, and massive volumes of data, they will have the capacity to go beyond the traditional ways of performance evaluation and start down the path toward proactive management and strategic expansion (Shubhabrata Basu, Bishakha Majumdar *et al.*, 2023, Steven McCartney, 2022). This will allow them to go beyond the limitations of the past. During the course of this inquiry, we will look at case studies that are based on the real world, delve into the underlying ideas that drive predictive modeling, and discover the numerous challenges and ethical considerations that are associated with the use of this approach. When it is all said and done, the objective of this paper is to ensure that the reader has a comprehensive understanding of how anticipating employee performance may change the landscape of human resource management, cultivate a culture of excellence, and ultimately contribute to the long-term success of a firm.

Key Components of Predicting Employee Performance

Predicting employee performance using predictive models involves leveraging data and statistical techniques to forecast an employee's future performance based on historical patterns and various factors (Boudreau, J. W., & Cascio, W. F., 2017, Patrick Coolen, Sjoerd van den Heuvel *et al.*, 2023). Here are the key components involved in using predictive models for this purpose:

Data Collection and Preparation

Gather relevant data about employees, such as job skills, education, experience, performance history, personality assessments, engagement surveys, *etc.* Make sure that the data is accurate and consistent by cleaning, preprocessing, and transforming it. Take care of missing data, unusual observations, and other data quirks that might hurt the model's accuracy.

Feature Selection and Engineering

Identify the most relevant features (variables) that are likely to influence employee performance. Create new features through engineering that might capture complex relationships in the data. Use domain knowledge and statistical analysis to select features that provide predictive power.

Model Selection

Based on the situation at hand and the information at hand, select the most suitable predictive modeling approach. Common methods include regression analysis, tree-based decision making, random forest sampling, gradient boost, neural networks, and so on. Consider the trade-offs between interpretability and predictive power when selecting models.

Model Training

Separate the data into a training set and a test set so that you can compare the two. Train the predictive model on the training data using the selected algorithm. Adjust hyper parameters of the model to optimize its performance.

Validation and Evaluation

Apply problem-specific measures like accuracy, precision, recall, F1-score, or area under the ROC curve (AUC-ROC) to assess the model's efficacy. Utilize cross-validation techniques to ensure the model's robustness and generalizability.

Feature Importance Analysis

Analyze the importance of different features in predicting employee performance using techniques like feature importance plots or permutation importance. Identify which features have the most significant impact on the model's predictions.

Model Interpretability

In some cases, knowing what informs the model's predictions is crucial. SHAP (Shapley Additive Explanations) and LIME (Local Interpretable Model-agnostic

Explanations) are two methods that can shed light on the reasoning behind model choices.

Deployment and Monitoring

Deploy the trained predictive model into a production environment where it can generate predictions for new data. Continuously monitor the model's performance and recalibrate or update it as needed to maintain accuracy over time.

Ethical Considerations

Ensure that the data used for training the model is representative and unbiased to avoid perpetuating any existing biases. Regularly assess the model for potential biases and take steps to mitigate them.

Iterative Improvement

Predictive models should be considered a work in progress. Continuously collect feedback, gather new data, and refine the model to enhance its predictive accuracy. Predictive modeling for employee performance is a dynamic process that requires collaboration between data scientists, HR professionals, and domain experts to create accurate and ethical models that benefit both employees and the organization.

The Importance of Predictive Employee Performance

Predicting employee performance using predictive models offers several important benefits for organizations (Li, Y., Yang, Y., & Xu, D., 2017; McCartney, S., & Van Dijk, R., 2016). These benefits can positively impact various aspects of the business, from talent management to overall productivity and success. Here are some key reasons highlighting the importance of predicting employee performance using predictive models:

Informed Decision-Making

Predictive models provide data-driven insights that help organizations make informed decisions about employee hiring, promotion, development, and retention. These insights are based on historical patterns and current data, reducing reliance on intuition alone.

Talent Acquisition

Predictive models assist in identifying the right candidates during the hiring process by evaluating their potential fit for the role and the organization. This leads to more efficient recruitment and a higher likelihood of hiring employees who excel in their roles.

Resource Allocation

Accurate performance predictions guide organizations in allocating resources effectively. By identifying high-performing employees, organizations can focus on nurturing and developing talent that drives the most significant impact.

Strategic Workforce Planning

Predictive models enable organizations to plan for future workforce needs by understanding which roles are likely to require additional resources and which employees are best suited for leadership positions.

Personalized Development

Predictive models help tailor individualized development plans for employees based on their strengths, weaknesses, and potential. This ensures that training and development efforts are aligned with employee growth trajectories.

Employee Engagement

When employees see that their skills and contributions are recognized and nurtured, their engagement and job satisfaction tend to increase. Predictive models facilitate targeted engagement strategies by focusing on each employee's unique needs.

Retention Strategies

Identifying employees at risk of leaving the organization allows for the implementation of proactive retention strategies. This could include personalized incentives, career growth opportunities, or addressing specific concerns.

Performance Metrics Alignment

Predictive models help align performance metrics with business goals and objectives, ensuring that employees' efforts contribute to the organization's overall success.

Reduced Turnover Costs

Accurate predictions of employee performance lead to better retention rates. This reduces turnover costs associated with recruitment, training, and lost productivity.

Effective Succession Planning

Organizations can identify potential successors for critical roles in advance, ensuring a smooth transition when current leaders step down or move to new positions.

Predicting employee performance using predictive models empowers organizations to optimize their workforce, improve decision-making, enhance employee satisfaction, and achieve greater business success. It fosters a data-driven culture where talent is strategically managed to meet current and future challenges.

Integration of Predicting Employee Performance and Predictive Models

The integration of predicting employee performance using predictive models involves incorporating data-driven insights into various aspects of talent management and organizational decision-making. This integration requires a systematic approach to ensure that predictive models are effectively utilized to optimize employee performance and organizational success (Edwards, M., 2019; Laxmi Pandit Vishwakarma, Rajesh Kumar Singh, 2023). Here's how the integration process can be approached:

Data Collection and Management

Gather and organize relevant employee data, including skills, experience, performance metrics, feedback, and any other pertinent information. Ensure data quality, consistency, and security to create a reliable foundation for predictive modeling.

Model Development and Validation

Develop predictive models that are tailored to the organization's specific needs, considering factors such as job roles, performance metrics, and available data. Train and validate the models using historical data to ensure they accurately predict employee performance.

Integration into HR Processes

Embed predictive insights into HR processes such as recruitment, onboarding, performance evaluation, career development, and succession planning. Use predictive models to identify high-potential candidates during the hiring process and tailor development plans for existing employees.

Talent Acquisition and Recruitment

Applying predictive models to the hiring process can help you find the people who are most suited to the open positions and the company's culture. Select applicants based on objective criteria to get the greatest possible match between skills and needs.

Performance Management

Incorporate predictive performance metrics into regular evaluations to provide a comprehensive view of employee contributions. Identify areas for improvement and create targeted development plans based on predictive insights.

Succession Planning

Identify employees with the potential to fill key leadership positions using predictive models. Develop and nurture a pipeline of talent by providing the necessary training and experiences to prepare them for future roles.

Employee Development

Design personalized development plans for employees based on their predicted strengths, weaknesses, and growth trajectories. Offer relevant training, mentorship, and opportunities that align with each employee's unique needs.

Retention Strategies

Use predictive insights to identify employees at risk of leaving the organization and implement retention strategies tailored to their individual needs. Address concerns and provide incentives that align with employees' motivations and goals.

Continuous Improvement

Continuously assess the performance of predictive models, refine them based on new data and changing circumstances, and enhance their accuracy over time. Gather feedback from HR professionals and managers to fine-tune the models and optimize their utility.

Leadership Support and Training

Ensure that HR professionals and managers understand how to interpret and utilize predictive insights effectively. Provide training on the integration of predictive models into existing HR processes.

Ethical Considerations

Regularly evaluate the models for potential biases and take steps to address any disparities in predictions. Ensure transparency in how predictive insights are used to make decisions about employees' careers and opportunities.

Communication and Transparency

Communicate with employees about the use of predictive models in performance management, ensuring transparency and addressing any concerns. The successful integration of predictive models into employee performance management requires a collaborative effort between HR professionals, data scientists, managers, and leadership. By aligning data-driven insights with HR processes, organizations can optimize talent management strategies, enhance employee development, and achieve better business outcomes.

Implementing Predictive Employee Performance in an Organization

Implementing a predictive employee performance system within an organization requires careful planning, coordination, and a phased approach (Gururama Senthilvel, Duraimutharasan, *et al.*, 2023). Here's a step-by-step guide to help you successfully implement predicting employee performance using predictive models:

Define Objectives and Goals

Clearly articulate the goals and objectives of implementing predictive employee performance. Are you aiming to improve hiring, development, retention, or all of the above?

Assemble a Cross-Functional Team

Form a team with members from HR, data science, IT, and relevant business units to collaborate on the implementation.

Data Gathering and Preparation

Collect and clean relevant employee data, including performance metrics, skills, experience, and any other data points that could contribute to predictions.

Choose Predictive Models

Select appropriate predictive models based on the nature of your data and objectives. This could involve regression, decision trees, neural networks, or other machine learning techniques.

Successful implementation requires ongoing commitment, flexibility, and a willingness to adapt based on the evolving needs of the organization and its workforce (Shanti Devi Chhetri, Devesh Kumar, Deepesh Ranabhat, 2023). By following these steps and involving relevant stakeholders, you can create a predictive employee performance system that enhances talent management and contributes to organizational success (María J. Belizón, Sarah Kieran, 2021).

CASE STUDIES

Case Study 1

Tech Startup Talent Optimization

A fast-growing tech startup is looking to optimize its talent management strategies. They want to identify high-potential candidates during the recruitment process, tailor development plans for existing employees, and reduce turnover. Gather data on employee skills, experience, education, performance metrics, and engagement surveys. Choose a machine learning algorithm that can predict performance based on historical data. Create features like technical skills, years of experience, educational background, and self-reported goals. Train the predictive model using historical performance data as the target variable. Validate the model's accuracy using cross-validation techniques. Integrate the predictive model into the hiring process to Use predictive insights to tailor personalized development plans for employees, focusing on their predicted strengths and areas for improvement. The startup successfully identifies top-performing candidates during recruitment, leading to more effective hires and reduced turnover. Tailored development plans boost employee satisfaction, engagement, and performance.

Case Study 2

Retail Chain Employee Succession Planning

A large retail chain wants to implement a succession planning strategy to identify employees with leadership potential and prepare them for future managerial roles. Gather employee data, including job history, performance evaluations, training records, and self-assessment surveys. Build a predictive model that uses historical data to identify employees likely to excel in leadership roles. Select features such as past performance, time with the company, and feedback from peers and managers. Train the model using historical successions and performance outcomes. Validate the model's predictions against actual managerial successions. Implement the model to proactively identify employees with leadership potential and provide them with relevant training and opportunities. Continuously monitor the effectiveness of the model in identifying potential leaders and the success of their career progression. The retail chain successfully identifies and grooms potential leaders, reducing the risk of leadership gaps and ensuring a smooth transition when managerial roles need to be filled.

Case Study 3

Financial Services Performance Enhancement

A financial services company aims to enhance employee performance and retention by predicting potential performance issues and addressing them proactively. Collect employee data, including performance metrics, engagement surveys, workload, and feedback. Develop a predictive model to identify employees at risk of underperformance or leaving the organization. Create features such as recent performance trends, work hours, and job satisfaction scores. Train the model using historical performance data and exit records. Set up an alert system that notifies managers when an employee's predicted performance or engagement drops below a certain threshold. Managers use predictive insights to engage with at-risk employees, offer support, and create improvement plans. Continuously analyze the effectiveness of the model in preventing performance issues and reducing turnover. The financial services company experiences improved employee satisfaction, engagement, and performance by proactively addressing potential issues, resulting in enhanced organizational productivity and retention rates.

CONCLUSION

Predicting employee performance using predictive models is a transformative approach that empowers organizations to leverage data-driven insights for optimized talent management. As we conclude, it is evident that this methodology offers a host of benefits that shape the future of HR practices and organizational success. By harnessing the power of historical data, advanced algorithms, and machine learning techniques, predictive models enable organizations to make informed decisions at every stage of the employee lifecycle. From recruitment and development to retention and succession planning, these models offer a comprehensive view of employee potential and contribution. The integration of predictive models into HR processes fosters efficiency, accuracy, and fairness. It facilitates the identification of high-potential candidates, personalizes development plans, and even helps in mitigating potential performance issues. The models enhance decision-making by moving beyond intuition, ensuring that strategies align with both individual employee aspirations and broader business objectives. However, the implementation of predictive models requires careful consideration of ethical implications, transparency, and ongoing refinement. Ensuring data privacy, addressing bias, and maintaining open communication are essential aspects of a successful deployment. In conclusion, predicting employee performance through predictive models marks a significant leap forward in HR innovation. By embracing this data-driven approach, organizations can tap into the full potential of their workforce, foster a culture of continuous improvement, and achieve remarkable outcomes that benefit both employees and the organization as a whole. In an era where data reigns, predictive models offer the roadmap to unlocking the full spectrum of employee performance, enabling organizations to thrive in an ever-evolving landscape.

REFERENCES

Shubhabrata Basu, Bishakha Majumdar *et al* (2023), Artificial Intelligence – HRM Interactions and Outcomes: A Systematic Review and Causal Configurational Explanation *Human Resource Management Review, 33*(1), 100893.
[http://dx.doi.org/10.1016/j.hrmr.2022.100893]

Boudreau, J., Cascio, W. (2017). Human capital analytics: why are we not there? *Journal of Organizational Effectiveness: People and Performance, 4*(2), 119-126.
[http://dx.doi.org/10.1108/JOEPP-03-2017-0021]

Coolen Patrick, Sjoerd van den Heuvel *et al* (2023), Understanding the adoption and institutionalization of workforce analytics: A systematic literature review and research agenda *Human Resource Management Review, 33*(4), 100985.
[http://dx.doi.org/10.1016/j.hrmr.2023.100985]

Chhetri, S.D., Kumar, D., Ranabhat, D. (2023). Investigating research in human resource analytics through the lens of systematic literature review. *Hum. Syst. Manag.,* 1-17.
[http://dx.doi.org/10.3233/HSM-230004]

Cascio, W.F. (2006). The economic impact of employee behaviors on organizational performance. *Calif. Manage. Rev., 48*(4), 41-59.
[http://dx.doi.org/10.1177/000812560604800401]

Chowdhury S, Hioe E, and Schaninger B (2018), Harnessing the Power of Performance Management, McKinsey & Company, Available from: www.mckinsey.com.

Edwards, M. (2019). Predictive HR Analytics: Mastering the HR Metric. HR Insights, Available from: https://www.hrinsights.com/predictive-hr-analytics.

Fulmer, I.S., Ployhart, R.E. (2014). Our Most Important Asset. *J. Manage., 40*(1), 161-192.
[http://dx.doi.org/10.1177/0149206313511271]

Laxmi Pandit Vishwakarma, Rajesh Kumar Singh (2023), An Analysis of the Challenges to Human Resource in Implementing Artificial Intelligence. *The Adoption and Effect of Artificial Intelligence on Human Resources Management, Part B,* 81-109.
[http://dx.doi.org/10.1108/978-1-80455-662-720230006]

Li, Y., Yang, Y., Xu, D. (2017). Predicting Employee Performance: A Multimodal Approach. *Journal of Human Resources Management., 45*(3), 225-242.
[http://dx.doi.org/10.1234/jhrm.2017.001]

María, J. (2021). Human resources analytics: A legitimacy process *Human Resource Management Journal, 3*(2), 603-630.
[http://dx.doi.org/10.1111/1748-8583.12417]

McCartney, S., Van Dijk, R. (2016). *Predictive Analytics for Human Resources.* Wiley and SAS Business Series.

Olaniyi, Olusegun Abayomi (2021), Employees Development and Productivity in Private Organization.

Available at SSRN: https://ssrn.com/abstract=3870417.
[http://dx.doi.org/10.2139/ssrn.3870417]

Steven McCartney (2022), Na Fu, Bridging the gap: why, how and when HR analytics can impact organizational performance *Management Decision, 60*(13), 25-47.
[http://dx.doi.org/10.1108/MD-12-2020-1581]

Senthilvel, G. (2023). Artificial Intelligence enabled Employee Performance Prediction using Comprehensive Learning Metrics *International Conference on Advances in Computing, Communication and Applied Informatics (ACCAI),* 1-7.

A Numbers Game or a People Game: An Analytical Approach to Bring the Best Talent to the Organizations

Rupa Rathee[1,*] and **Madhvi Lamba**[2,*]

[1] *Deenbandhu Chhotu Ram University of Science and Technology, Murthal, Haryana, India*

[2] *Department of Management Studies, Deenbandhu Chhotu Ram University of Science and Technology, Murthal, Haryana, 131039, India*

Abstract: Human resources analytics (HR analytics) is an interesting field of study for those who love to play with numbers. Playing with numbers seems fun, but the quantified data helps organizations in many ways. Do you want to go a long way in your business? Then, yes! HR analytics is for you. HR analytics deals with interpreting data by applying statistical tools in order to get meaningful information so that predictive analysis for the growth of an organization can be done. The modern concept of HR is more data-driven, and HR analytics provide an opportunity for organizations to follow data-driven approach in order to manage people. HR analytics can be applied to numerous functions of HR, but this chapter will specifically cover the concept of HR analytics by emphasizing more on talent management analytics and its aspects. Are you looking for the best talent in the market? Do you want to get qualitative people in minimum costs and time? Then, this chapter will help you by elaborating on numerous recruitment metrics and suggesting how talent management analytics can help in managing people and enhancing an organization's profitability. Moreover, this chapter also provides theoretical and practical insights to the readers to enhance their understanding with the help of numerical interpretations.

Keywords: Application, Candidate, Cost, Data, Decision, Employees, Hiring, HR analytics, Human, Human resources, Management, Metrics, People, Process, Quality, Recruitment, Strategies, Talent, Talent management, Technology.

INTRODUCTION

Is human capital investment still a thought-provoking term for organizations? The traditional approach hardly emphasizes human resources (HR) professionals in

---
* **Corresponding authors Rupa Rathee and Madhvi Lamba:** Deenbandhu Chhotu Ram University of Science and Technology, Murthal, Haryana, India; Department of Management Studies, Deenbandhu Chhotu Ram University of Science and Technology, Murthal, Haryana, 131039, India; E-mails: ruparathee18@gmail.com, lambamadhvi7@gmail.com

any profitable aspect for organizations. Why so? There is a probability that HR may not have strong skill sets in HR metrics and analytics. This again leads to the lack of decision-making competencies. Awareness of the right set of analytical models can also be another reason. Identifying the models that predict the association and gap between current HR practices and future HR practices may require the help of analytical models. But, is the perception of HR professionals the same even in the present era? The profession of HR has now shifted towards the strategic and decision-making side. HR analytics also helps in that particular aspect. People usually think the role of HR is merely recruiting and preparing the salaries of the employees. But is it so? Knowing a recruiter needs to hire people does not end the role of HR. This is just a traditional aspect of one of the roles of HR (recruitment), but knowing the turn around time (TAT), sourcing channels, their costs and effectiveness, cost per hire, efficiency of recruiter, satisfaction of hiring manager, and quality of hire will give facts and figures. These facts and figures will help in providing data to analyze, decide, and help in preparing future strategies by understanding the loopholes. By having an understanding of the loopholes, strategies can be formed to fill the gaps. This is how costs and time taken to hire candidates can be minimized. The quality of candidates can be improvised if required. The efficiency of the recruiter can be measured and enhanced by improvising the weaker areas.

It has been seen in the past decade that most organizations are moving towards the data-driven approach. The formation of strategies can be done with the help of the best decisions management can take. The amalgamation of data along with analytics is gaining the wider attention of professionals and researchers. The decisions can be made only on the basis of data analysis. Data can be prepared with a number of observations that come with the passage of time. This is where HR analytics comes into play. The profession of HR is shifting from a traditional approach to a more strategic and decision-making-oriented approach. Data analysis is also bringing revolution to the domain of HR as data is helping organizations to change for the better.

The human resource department is one of the most critical departments of the organization. Beyond recruitment and salary preparation, HR looks after the multiple functions of the HR gamut. The roles may include documentation, preparation of letters (offer, appointment, appraisal, increment and termination, *etc.*), attendance and leave management, employee engagement, training and development, compensation and salary, performance appraisal, employees' grievances, exit management, and other administrative activities. But this chapter will cover the analytics on talent management, majorly on the recruitment aspect. These terminologies may seem very simple, but when one dives into them, it gets wider with the data, which helps smoothen the process. These traditional practices, along with data analysis, have completely emerged as a whole new subject of HR analytics.

When the term "talent management" pops up, it usually means managing talent. That is correct. But how? Talent management consists of various roles such as recruiting, hiring, training, learning, developing, and retaining employees. Considering the depth of the individual aspects of talent management, this chapter will emphasize the recruitment facet of talent management. Besides recruitment, the chapter will be initiated with a brief overview of HR analytics. In order to understand each aspect of recruitment metrics and analytics, it is important to know about talent management and HR analytics.

So now, let us understand what HR analytics is?

HR ANALYTICS

Numbers, data, statistical tools, and reports result in successful outcomes in HR analytics when such data is used in the decision-making process.

Kryscynski *et al.* (2017) and Margherita (2020) described HR analytics as "data, metrics, statistics, and scientific methods, with the help of technology, to gauge the impact of human capital management practices on business goals."

According to van den Heuvel and Bondarouk (2017), Margherita (2020), and McCartney & Fu (2022), "HR analytics is the systematic identification and quantification of the people drivers of business outcomes to make better decisions."

Another definition by Mishra *et al.* (2016) and Margherita (2020) states, "HR analytics is a multidisciplinary approach to integrate methodologies for improving the quality of people-related decisions."

According to Deloitte, HR analytics revolves around four elements: information, process, technology, and people.

The keen interest in HR analytics revolves around four elements that are depicted in Fig. (**1**).

According to Lawler *et al.* (2004), HR analytics that provide valuable outcomes for businesses can be done in the following three steps:

• Identifying human resources metrics (HR metrics).
• Analytical model.

- Measurements of the performance of the company.

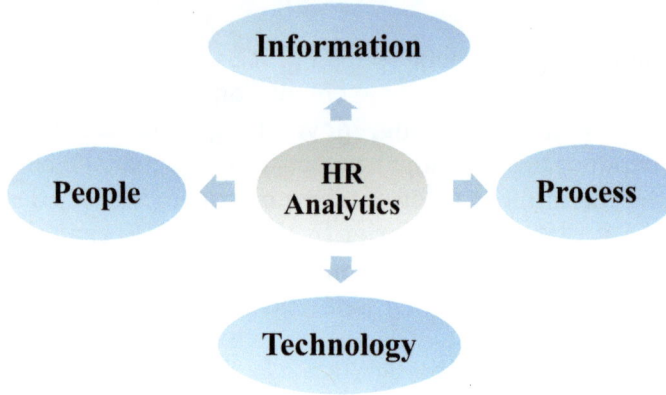

Fig. (1). Elements of HR analytics.

Fig. (**2**) depicts the three steps of HR analytics according to Lawler *et al.* (2004).

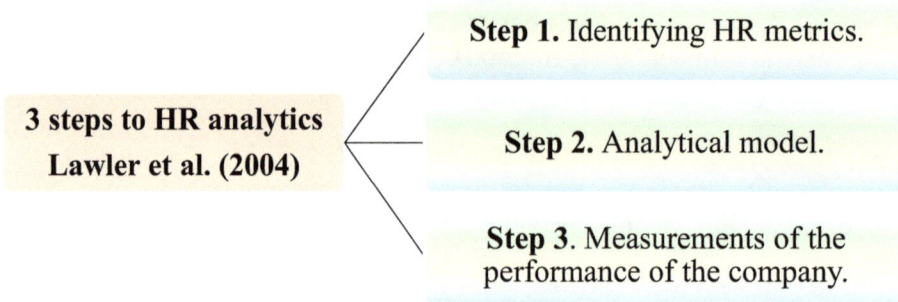

Fig. (2). Steps of HR analytics.

Lawler *et al.* (2004) differentiated the HR metrics from HR analytics. According to them, the metrics can be measured in the following three ways:

- Effectiveness
- Efficiency
- Impact

In order to identify the metrics of the organization, one needs to measure the efficiency, effectiveness, and impact (Fig. **3**).

According to Marler & Boudreau (2017), HR analytics is "an HR practice enabled by information technology that use descriptive, visual and statistical analyses of data related to HR processes, human capital, organizational performance, and external economic benchmarks to establish business impact on data-driven decision-making."

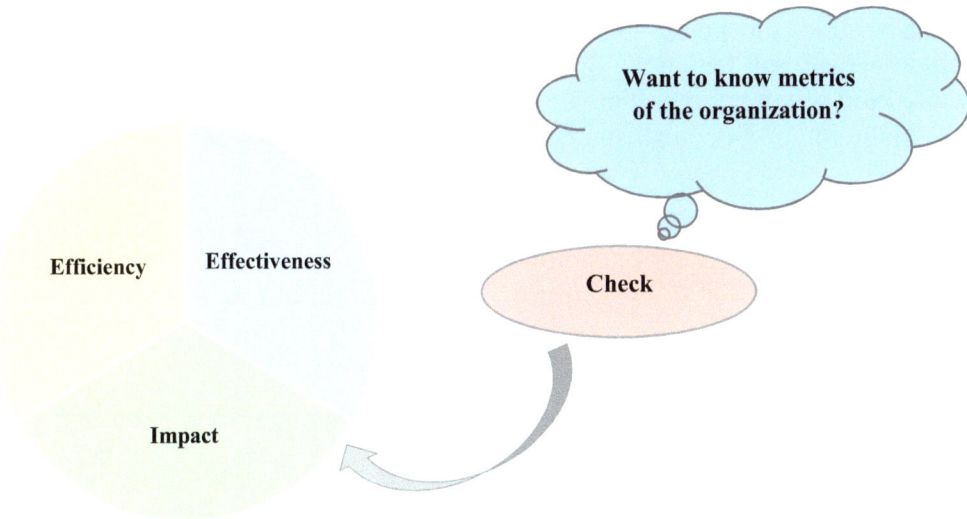

Fig. (3). Metrics of the organization.

SPHERES OF IMPLICATIONS OF ANALYTICS IN HR

HR is a vast domain. A limited number of HRs usually handle all the functions in startups or beginner-level organizations. But, when it comes to mid-level or big organizations, one HR cannot perform all the activities. So, such organizations bifurcate the activities of the HR gamut into different specializations. Therefore, there is a high level of possibility that the department and specialist are further segregated into various functions of HR: "recruiter" for "recruitment", "coordinator or operations specialist or generalist" for "HR operations", "payroll specialist" for "salary and payroll processing", "trainer or learning & development (L&D) expert" for "training, learning & development", *etc*. The components of these functions come under the subject of HR analytics when the analysis is done on the data of respective functions. As the data grows, so do the organizations and their requirement for human resources. How a qualitative hire with minimum time and cost can be done? What is the attrition rate in the last one year? This chapter will help you identify numbers related to recruitment metrics with the help of which important decisions can be made.

TALENT MANAGEMENT

First of all, let us understand the meaning of talent management. The concept of talent management emerged with the idea of human capital planning and employment. Majorly, it is considered that an article by consultants of McKinsey in 2001, "The War for Talent", has emphasized the concept of talent management.

Talent exhibits the possession of strategic capabilities. Such capabilities may include behavioral, technical, or any other special skill. Talent can be identified by any kind of potential, which allows an individual to grow and accomplish big tasks in the future. So, talent can be identified by following questions:

- Are you a future leader?
- Do you have any strategic capability?
- Is there any scope for you to achieve big tasks in the future?

Everyone has a talent. So, talent management includes everyone.

Talent management is all about planning, recruiting, training, developing, and retaining talented personnel.

According to the definitions given by numerous authors, the main aim of the organizations is to maximize the profits. For those profits, organizations want to keep their resources at a minimum cost so that more revenue can be generated. Talent management is a tool that allows for minimizing the cost of new hiring by retaining the talented resources in the organization. This is how they retain the experiences, skills, knowledge, insights, and capabilities of talented employees.

Talent management is also described as the addition of experiences, capabilities, attitudes, competencies, and behavior of the employees, which can be turned into the performance of the organization.

The article by consultants of McKinsey also emphasized the vitality of talent management:

- Establish a talent mindset throughout the entire organization, beginning at the top.
- Creation of a robust recruiting strategy.
- Creation of unique and leveraged value propositions for employees.
- Development and elevation of talent in an aggressive manner.
- Differentiate and affirm your employees

Why human capital is important?

Human capital is an amalgamation of various intangible elements like experience, skills, knowledge, competencies, and motivation. The growth and competitive spirit of the organization are based on the productivity and performance of the human capital. An uncertain, complex, and unpredictable environment requires the knowledge and insights of talented employees to sustain themselves in the business market. This is where the requirement for talented human capital comes in.

Talent Management Analytics

In talent management analytics, there are three major aspects of HR. These are as follows:

- Talent Management
- Training, Learning, and Development
- Retention and Turnover

In this chapter, talent management will be covered majorly, along with retention and turnover.

Recruitment

Is your organization looking for a candidate? Do you want a candidate with the right set of skills and expertise within little time as possible? The process of recruitment is considered a very rigorous process of looking out for a candidate with the requisite skills, experience, and competencies at the right place and at the right time so that the vacant position can be filled. But is recruitment restricted to this process only?

- Recruitment begins when the department that has a vacancy shares the job description with the hiring manager.
- The hiring manager looks for candidates through various sources: Job posting, liasioning, advertisement, on-campus hiring, walk-ins, job portals, *etc*.
- The candidates go through a screening round, which is also known as the preliminary round.
- The technical rounds and other requisite rounds are introduced to understand the technical capabilities of the candidates.
- The HR round and salary negotiations come into place after all such conversations.
- Prior to employment, candidates might be asked for amedical examination to understand if they are healthy as per the requirement of the role.
- Pre-employment verification or background verification can be done in many ways.
- After all the processes have been completed, the job for which the candidate has applied is offered to the candidate.

In between all these processes, most organizations follow recruitment and hiring analytics. The basis of recruitment and hiring analytics is the recruitment metrics. Data-driven recruitment, selection, and hiring can provide recruitment metrics.

It does not mean that all the organizations perform all the recruitment metrics. If the organizations will try to understand each and every recruitment metric, then no time will be left to do the actual task that is "recruitment".

Recruitment Metrics

Recruitment metrics are defined as tools that are used to gather the data, analyze it with the help of statistical tools, and make decisions by concluding the valuable information from the data. This tool allows the quantification of the data and prepares the recruiter to make better decisions in order to choose qualitative talent from the market.

Why is it important to get a quality candidate? The process of recruitment is expensive monetarily and non-monetarily. In order to hire good candidates, it takes time and cost. To enhance return on investment (ROI), metrics and analytics come into play.

Features of recruitment metrics:

- Actionable and predictive
- Consistent
- Benchmark to analyze internal performance.
- Qualitative hiring
- Return on investment

Following are the recruitment metrics (Table 1):

Applicants Per Opening

Applicants per job opening means how many applicants are there for the desired job role. There is a probability that a recruiter might be looking for candidates through various resources.

Application Completion Rate

Application completion rate is defined as the number of candidates who completed the job application process with respect to the total number of candidates who initiated the job application.

Table 1. Recruitment Metrics.

1. Applicants per opening	**10.** Offer acceptance rate
2. Application completion rate	**11.** Recruitment funnel effectiveness
3. Candidate call-back rate	**12.** Sourcing channel effectiveness
4. Source of hire	**13.** Sourcing channel costs
5. Time to fill	**14.** Recruiter performance metrics
6. Time to hire	**15.** Candidate experience
7. Selection ratio	**16.** Hiring manager satisfaction
8. Quality of hire	**17.** Retention rate
9. Cost per hire	**18.** Attrition Rate

$$\text{Application completion rate (\%)} = \frac{\text{Total number of completed/submitted job application}}{\text{Total number of job application initiated}} \times 100$$

Example

Let us say an ABC organization has posted a job for the profile of human resource manager on their career page of the website. Around 1150 candidates have begun the process. Out of these, 850 candidates have submitted the application form. What is the application completion rate of the human resource manager?

$$\text{Application completion rate} = \frac{850}{1150} \times 100 = 73.9130\%.$$

This means that 73.91% of the applicants have completed the job application form for the profile of human resource manager at ABC organization.

This process, in reverse, can be used to identify the **application drop-off rate**. This value will define the number of candidates who began the application process but did not complete it. There can be various reasons for this, such as rigorous application process, incompatibility with the browser, and unamiable interface.

Candidate Call-back Rate

Candidate call-back rate is defined as the number of candidates who have called back the recruiter with respect to the candidates who have been asked for a call-back by the recruiter.

Candidate call back rate (%) = <u>Number of candidates who called back</u> X100

Total number of candidates asked
by recruiter to give a call back

Example

In order to understand the success of the pitching efforts of Ms. Sneha Chakarborty, Mr. Prashant Gautam has tried to measure the candidate call-back rate for the month of May. Ms. Sneha has called 2500 people in a month. Out of which, 1500 people have taken the call. After careful evaluation of the profile, 750 profiles have appealed to her, to whom she requested a call-back. Out of 750, 250 candidates have given her a call-back. What is the candidate call-back rate?

Candidate call back rate= <u>250</u> X 100 = 33.3333%

750

The calculated numbers exhibit that 33.33% of candidates have called Ms. Sneha back.

Source of Hire

Source of hire is an important metric to be measured. Source of hire is defined as the medium through which the candidates have been hired for the vacant positions. Furthermore, understanding which recruiting source is working best for hiring needs will lead the investment to the right place and enhance returns.

There are numerous ways to hire a candidate:

- Job boards: LinkedIn, Naukri, Indeed, Hirect, Instahire, Apnahire *etc.*
- Internal Job Postings (IJP).
- Campus recruitment drive.
- Walk-in interviews.
- Advertisement: Newspaper, Radio.
- Career page of the company.
- Sourcing agent or vendors.
- Job fairs.

How to understand which one works as the best source of hiring? This can be understood with the help of the recruitment metric "source of hire".

Let us take an example of a company that calculated the source of hire metric. The total number of candidates hired during the last year was 100. Out of these, 40 candidates were hired at the managerial level (40% of total hiring), whereas 60 candidates were hired at the executive level (60% of total hiring). Thirty candidates were hired through IJP (30% of total hiring), whereas 6 candidates were hired through LinkedIn (6% of total hiring) and 4 candidates through the career page of the company (4% of total hiring). At the executive level, 45 candidates were hired through the Naukri portal (45% of total hiring), whereas 8 candidates were hired through the campus recruitment drive (8% of total hiring), and 7 candidates were hired through job fairs (7% of total hiring).

The above example clearly shows that IJP worked well for the managerial level positions, whereas the Naukri portal worked best for the executive level positions.

Time to Fill

Time to fill is defined as the number of days taken between job posting and hiring of a new candidate. It helps in understanding the time it takes to fill a position or identify a replacement. A few factors can impact the time to fill, such as:

• The demand and supply ratio for particular job profiles.
• Time taken by the recruiter to fill a position for that specific profile.

Benefits of time to fill:

• Helps in efficient hiring planning.
• Provides warning alerts if the hiring process is getting too long.

Please note, that the time to fill the position may vary from organization to organization based on their own calculation.

How to calculate the average time to fill?

Let us assume in the past 6 months, a total of 5 candidates were hired for a specific role. The first candidate was hired in 45 days, the second in 32 days, the third in 37 days, the fourth in 50 days, and the fifth in 26 days. In order to calculate the average time period to fill that particular position, the number of days of all the hiring for that specific profile will be added and divided by total number of hiring.

$$\text{Average time to fill the position} = \frac{45 + 32 + 37 + 50 + 26}{5} = \frac{190}{5} = 38 \text{ days}$$

So, the average time to fill that particular role will be 38 days.

How do we minimize the time to fill?

- Creation of a database of the candidates.
- Creation of talent pipeline before the time.
- Creation of referral system.
- Job posting to colleagues.

These are the least expensive ways to create a talent pool.

Time to Hire

Time to hire or time to accept is one of the important recruitment metrics. It is the time span between the day the candidate applies for a job and the day the candidate accepts the offered job. According to some organizations, the calculation may extend up to the day on which the candidate gets on board.

It measures the number of days between the recruiting to hiring (R2H) process.

Time to hire may vary from one job role to another job role. It may also vary from the recruitment process of one organization to the recruitment process of another organization. For example, an organization may have three stages for the selection of a candidate, while another organization may have seven stages in their selection process. There is a high probability that the time to hire a candidate in an organization where there are seven stages will be more than an organization where there are three stages.

Time to hire also enablesus to understand which stage is taking less time and which one is taking more time. Thus, it can also help redefine recruiting strategies to minimize the time at the stage that is taking more.

Selection Ratio

The selection ratio is defined as a ratio of the number of candidates who have been offered a job role to the total number of candidates.

$$\text{Selection ratio} = \frac{\text{Number of candidates who have been offered for a job}}{\text{Total number of candidates}}$$

Example

There is a job opening for the profile of Business Analyst at XYZ Pvt. Ltd. The total number of applications received by the organization is 450. Out of which, 10 candidates were hired by XYZ Pvt. Ltd. Calculate the selection ratio.

$$\text{Selection ration} = \frac{10}{450} = 1{:}45$$

This example illustrates that among 45 applicants, 1 applicant was selected and offered a particular job . In simple words, 1 applicant was selected out of 45 applicants. Thus, 10 out of 450.

Quality of Hire

Quality of hire should be a quintessential metric for every organization. The measurement of quality of hire defines the value a new hire brings to the organization. This means that the quality of hire can be justified by evaluating the performance of the employee who has been hired lately (within a year).

$$\text{Quality of hire} = \frac{\text{Sum of all the indicators (Indicator 1\% + Indicator 2\% + ……+ Indicator n\%)}}{\text{Total number of indicators}}$$

Hiring success comes with high-rated employees based on their performance, whereas low-performance ratings emphasize exploring better recruiting strategies.

Numerous factors like management abilities, cultural fit, job fit, and retention can be different factors on which quality of hire can be measured.

Quality of hire can act as an input for the success ratio. The success ratio can be identified by dividing the number of new employees who have reached the desired performance benchmark by the total number of hires within a particular time span. Success ratio can be of two types:

• High success ratio
• Low success ratio

$$\text{Success ratio} = \frac{\text{Number of new employees who reached desired performance benchmark}}{\text{Total number of new hiring}}$$
$$(\text{calculation of desired time frame})$$

Example

A company hired 30 employees for the project management department in the past year. Out of 30, 24 performed well. Now, the company wants to understand the success ratio of new hiring. So, for that purpose, a company needs to calculate the success ratio by applying the above-mentioned formula.

$$\text{Success ratio} = \frac{24}{30} = 4{:}5$$

The outcomes show that 4 out of 5 employees have either reached the desired benchmark or performed extraordinarily, whereas 1 out of 5 employees has not reached the desired benchmark.

Why quality of hire is a quintessential factor?

- It leads to less attrition.
- More productivity can be attained.
- A better culture can be built.
- The company leads to success.
- Continuous measurement of these metrics can help in the improvisation of recruiting strategies as and when required.

Cost Per Hire

Cost per hire is defined as the total cost incurred to fill a vacant position. It can be identified by the sum of internal and external costs divided by the total number of hires.

Internal recruitment costs may include statutory compliances, training, learning and development expenses, administrative expenses, and recruiters' costs.

External recruitment costs may include commission (if hiring is through a vendor or other parties), background verification, medical verification, traveling, technological expenses, recruitment drives expenses, and advertisement costs.

$$\text{Cost per hire} = \frac{\text{Total internal costs} + \text{Total external costs}}{\text{Total number of hiring}}$$

(Total internal costs + Total external costs = Total recruitment costs)

Example

An organization needed to hire some executives. For that purpose, they tried to create a talent pool through various resources. With this, they could hire 8 candidates. The total internal cost for the entire process came out to be INR 9,000/-, whereas the total external cost came out to be INR 18000/-. What is the individual cost per hire?

$$\text{Cost per hire} = \frac{9000 + 18000}{8} = \frac{27000}{8} = 3375$$

The above calculation exhibits that the total cost per individual hiring was INR 3,375/-.

Offer Acceptance Rate

After the successful completion of interviews and other discussions, an offer letter is issued to the potential candidates. Some candidates may accept the offer letter by sharing the confirmation, whereas others may receive it but do not acknowledge the acceptance. So, the offer acceptance rate can be identified by dividing the number of candidates who accepted the offer by the total number of offer letters issued.

$$\text{Offer Acceptance Rate (\%)} = \frac{\text{Total number of offers accepted by candidates'}}{\text{Total number of offer letters rolled out by organization}} \times 100$$

Example

In order to understand the offer acceptance rate of quarter 1, XYZ Pvt. Ltd. conducted a study. The total number of offers rolled out for various positions was 30. The total number of candidates who accepted the offer was 17. So, what was the offer acceptance rate?

$$\text{Offer acceptance rate} = \frac{17}{30} \times 100 = 56.6667\%$$

The above calculation shows that 56.67% of the candidates accepted the job offer, whereas 43.33% of the candidates did not receive the job offer.

Recruitment Funnel Effectiveness

Recruitment is a process of scrutinizing candidates and identifying the well-fitted candidate as per the requirements of the organization. This process begins with the sourcing of the candidate and ends when the offer letter has been rolled out and accepted by the potential candidate.

Let us try to understand with the help of an example.

Do you know the effectiveness of each stage of your recruitment process? In order to understand that, the yield ratio must be identified. The yield ratio is defined as the percentage of candidates who move from one stage of the recruitment process to the other.

Yield ratio can be identified from one stage to the next stage as well as from the first stage to the last stage.

In order to check the effectiveness of the first stage to the last stage, we will identify the yield ratio between the application received and the offer rolled out. It would be as follows:

$$= 20/1000 \text{ X } 100 = 2\%$$

Sourcing Channel Effectiveness

There are various ways to source a candidate, such as job boards, campus recruitment drives, walk-ins, job fairs, the career page of the company, social media, etc. Identifying which source works best to pick qualitative candidates is known as identifying sourcing channel effectiveness.

This is simply about having the number of potential candidates from different sourcing channels.

To understand the sourcing channel effectiveness, calculate the number of applications received from specific channels in a time span and understand which channel is providing most of the applications.

Again, in order to understand which channel is providing the qualified and good candidates, calculate the qualitative applications received for the desired profile in the same time span.

What is the benefit of calculating sourcing channel effectiveness?

By calculating sourcing channel effectiveness, the information about which channel is producing quality data and which channels are not can be received. Based on the information, the expenses can be reduced by eliminating the channels that are not producing desirable outcomes.

Sourcing Channel costs

The sourcing channel cost can be calculated by dividing the total amount spent on advertisement per channel by the number of potential applicants per platform.

Sourcing channel cost = $\dfrac{\text{Total amount spent on advertisement per channel}}{\text{Number of potential candidate per platform}}$

Example

A company posted a job opening for a pre-sales manager on LinkedIn. The job posting might have costed INR 500/- to that company. With this job post, the company could find 25 relevant profiles. What would be the sourcing channel cost for the profile of the pre-sales manager?

$$\text{Sourcing channel cost} = \frac{500}{25} = 20$$

This means that the sourcing channel cost is INR 20/- per candidate.

Recruiter Performance Metrics

Do you know how your recruiter is performing? The job of a recruiter includes sourcing through various modes, pitching, screening, connecting with concerned departments, hiring managers for interviews, and negotiating and releasing offers.

This can be identified by various means, such as how much time a recruiter is taking to fill the position. Is it less, or is it too long? How many candidates are selected for the interview? Is the recruiter looking for quality or quantity? How many candidates who are offered the job join the organization? Is your recruiter able to engage them appropriately?

Candidate Experience

Candidate experience is defined as the way a candidate perceives the entire recruiting process. Candidates' experience can be measured by various surveys using different kinds of scales.

Hiring Manager Satisfaction

A term mentioned above, quality of hire, can be one of the trustable metrics to identify the satisfaction of the hiring manager. If a hiring manager is satisfied with the new hire, the new hire will be more likely to perform as per or better than the set benchmark and can be a fine fit in the organization.

Retention Rate

Retention rate is defined as the ability of the organization to sustain employees for a longer period of time.

Attrition Rate

This is a vital metric that need to be measured by every organization. The attrition rate is defined as when employees leave the organization either voluntarily or involuntarily.

Voluntary attrition means the employee has left the organization by his/her own willingness.

Involuntary attrition means the employee has been asked by the employer to leave the organization or terminated on some grounds. This kind of attrition states that the quality of hiring was not good.

The attrition rate, specifically during the first year of the job role, is considered bad.

Now, let us understand how to calculate the attrition rate?

Example

An organization was started in 2018 and is growing slowly. Although new people are joining the organization, a few are leaving as well. The management of the organization wants to understand the reason behind the attrition. For that purpose, they need data on how much attrition was there in Q1 of 2023. Following is the data for Q1:

Total number of employees in 01.04.2023 (Open) = 50

Total new joining (New Joiner) = 10

Total employees left (Left) = 4

Calculate attrition.

In order to calculate the attrition rate, first of all, the total number of employees on 30.06.2023 will be calculated.

$$\text{Total employees (Closed)} = (\text{Open} + \text{New Joiner}) - \text{Left}$$

$$= (50 + 10) - 4 = 56$$

Now, the average number of employees will be calculated in Q1. The number of employees in each month might not be same. So, the average number of employees working in Q1 will be identified. To calculate, the average number of employees open and closed will be added and divided by 2.

$$\text{Average} = \frac{\text{Open} + \text{Closed}}{2}$$

$$= \frac{50 + 56}{2} = 58$$

To calculate the attrition rate, divide the number of employees who left by the average number of employees.

$$\text{Attrition rate} = \frac{\text{Left employees}}{\text{Average employees}} \times 100$$

Left employees in Q1 = 4.

Average employees in Q1 = 58.

Attrition rate in Q1= (4/58) X 100= 6.89%

This means the attrition rate of Q1 is 6.89%, which is nearly equal to 7%.

To get the attrition rate for the last year, HR must have the requisite data for the last year. The attrition rate can be identified by applying the above-mentioned formula.

The formulas used in this chapter are taken from different resources and mentioned in the references.

How Talent Management Analytics can Help in People Management?

Talent management covers the process of recruitment, training, learning, development, and retention. Some metrics and data are required to understand the following regarding talent management:

- Data about the employees.
- Efficiency and effectiveness of the process associated with talent management.
- Degree of cultural and environmental support.

Measurement includes the following parameters:

- Set goals
- Track progress.
- Benchmark internally/externally/link if possible.

Some major benefits are:

- In order to attain effectiveness and efficiency in the process of recruitment, recruitment metrics are used.
- It provides vital information in a quantified and meaningful manner. Strategic decision-making can be done easily based on such data.

- By applying the analytical and strategic approach in the process of recruitment, qualitative hiring can be done, and those employees can be retained for a longer period of time. The hiring can be done by aligning the vision, mission and goal of the organization with that of the candidate.
- It also supports improving HR-associated processes. The data provides credibility and consistency. It gives the pointers that can do wonders in what-if scenarios.
- It allows the effective and efficient usage of minimal resources with meaningful outcomes for the organization.

CONCLUSION

As analytics is applied to data in various fields, HR is also getting vast with subjects like HR analytics. According to us, HR analytics for any organization is defined as the analysis of data for the people of the organization. Information, people, process, and technology are the key components of HR analytics. HR analytics can be applied to various processes of end-to-end employee life cycles, but this chapter covers one aspect of HR, which is talent management. As talent management is seen as an amalgamation of three components, recruitment is the major component, which has been detailed in the chapter. A total of 18 recruitment metrics have been discussed in the chapter. By understanding various recruitment metrics, meaningful information can be interpreted. These metrics can help in attaining effectiveness and efficiency in the process of recruitment. Understanding where the costs need to be minimized can contribute to organizational profitability, as organizations will have meaningful resources at minimum cost. Numerical data has authenticity, credibility and reliability. It enables the organizations to understand the positive and negative aspects of the processes. This enhances decision making and strategy planning in a better and more authentic way. By identifying loopholes, decisions can be made, improvised, and restructured accordingly.

REFERENCES

Adriyanto, A.T. (2020). Enhancing Job Satisfaction through Colleague Support and Communication *Proceedings of the 4th International Conference on Sustainable Innovation 2020-Accounting and Management (ICoSIAMS 2020), Advances in Economics, Business and Management Research, Atlantis Press, 176*, 222-228.

Dalahmeh, M.A. (2020). Talent Management: A Systematic Review, *Oradea. J. Bus. Econ., 5.*

Dziuba, S.T., Ingaldi, M., Zhuravskaya, M. (2020). Employees' Job Satisfaction and their Work Performance as Elements Influencing Work Safety. *CzOTO, 2*(1), 18-25.
[http://dx.doi.org/10.2478/9788395720437-003]

D., Reeves, C., Stice-Lusvardi, R., Ulrich, M., & Russell, G. (2017). Analytical abilities and the performance of HR professionals, Human Resource Management, 57(3), 715–738.

DV Prasad, K., Rao, M., Vaidya, R. (2019). Recruitment metrics and accomplishments: A study with reference to information technology sector. *Journal of Management Research and Analysis, 6*(2), 106-111. [http://dx.doi.org/10.18231/j.jmra.2019.020]

Gould, A. (n.d.), HR Metrics Checklist, Human Resources Analytics [MOOC]. Coursera: Available from: https://hrlens.org/wp-content/uploads/2019/11/HR-Metrics-Checklist.pdf.

HR Analytics, Deloitte, Retrieved on 18.05.2023, Available from: https://www2.deloitte.com/be/en/pages/accountancy/articles/hr-analytics.html.

Lawler, E.E., III, Levenson, A., Boudreau, J.W. (2004). HR metrics and analytics: Use and Impact. *Human Resource Planning, 27*, 27-35.

Margherita, A. (2022). Human resources analytics: A systematization of research topics and directions for future research. *Hum. Resour. Manage. Rev., 32*(2), 100795. [http://dx.doi.org/10.1016/j.hrmr.2020.100795]

Marler, J.H., Boudreau, J.W. (2017). An evidence-based review of HR Analytics. *Int. J. Hum. Resour. Manage., 28*(1), 3-26. [http://dx.doi.org/10.1080/09585192.2016.1244699]

Mayo, A. (2018). Applying HR analytics to talent management. *Strategic HR Rev., 17*(5), 247-254. [http://dx.doi.org/10.1108/SHR-08-2018-0072]

McCartney, S. & Fu, N. (2022), Bridging the gap: why, how and when HR analytics can impact organizational performance, Emerald Publishing Limited, 60 (13), 25-47. [http://dx.doi.org/10.1108/MD-12-2020-1581]

Michaels, E., Handfield-Jones, H. and Axelrod, B., 2001. The war for talent. 1st Ed., London: Harvard Business Press.

Mishra, S.N., Lama, D.R., Pal, Y. (2016). Human resource predictive analytics (HRPA) for HR management in organizations. *International Journal of Scientific and Technology Research, 5*(5), 33-35.

Recruiting Metrics CheatSheet, LinkedIn. Retrieved on 20.05.2023, Available from: https://business.linkedin.com/talent-solutions/recruiting-tips/recruiting-metrics-cheat-sheet.

Van den Heuvel, S., Bondarouk, T. (2017). The rise (and fall?) of HR analytics. *Journal of Organizational Effectiveness: People and Performance, 4*(2), 157-178. [http://dx.doi.org/10.1108/JOEPP-03-2017-0022]

Vulpen, E. V. (2022), 21 Recruiting Metrics You Should Know About, Academy to Innovate HR, Available from: https://www.aihr.com/blog/recruiting-metrics/.

Vulpen, E. V., Yield Ratio: All You Need to Know, Academy to Innovate HR, Available from: https://www.aihr.com/blog/yield-ratio/.

CHAPTER 8

HR Analytics: Concept, Advantages and Obstacles

Jatinder Kaur[1,*] and **Srijan Gupta**[1]

[1] *Rukmini Devi Institute of Advanced Studies, Affilated to GGSIPU, New Delhi, India*

Abstract: In the contemporary landscape, the management of employees within organizations has transformed into a collaborative endeavor. The responsibility for managing personnel and evaluating their performance has moved to online platforms, made possible by the integration of HR analytic tools in light of changing company dynamics and technological advancement. The strategic use of HR analytics (HRA) has been shown to be essential for improving employee performance and increasing operational effectiveness. Noteworthy improvements have been witnessed in critical areas such as recruitment quality, talent management, employee productivity, and the reduction of employee turnover.

The focal point of this research centers on an in-depth exploration of HR analytics, encompassing its multifaceted tools and their diverse applications across distinct organizational contexts. The main goal is to identify the numerous advantages of the wise application of HRA. Through the lens of logical tools, organizations gain the acumen to identify and address pertinent issues, including performance disparities, employee attrition, retention challenges, and nuanced employee behaviors, leveraging the troves of data inherent within the organizational framework.

This study has been instigated in response to the prevalent underestimation of HR's potential within numerous organizations. Despite this underestimation, the modern technological milieu has borne an array of analytical tools, which have garnered considerable adoption by major corporate entities. Within the confines of this paper, we delve into the illustrative cases of HR analytics implementation across five diverse organizations. Through empirical analysis, we discern how the strategic incorporation of HR analytics has yielded tangible benefits both for the organizations and their workforce, often resulting in transformative shifts towards a more people-centric business approach.

Keywords: Data metrics, Employee attrition, HR analytics, Organizational enhancement.

---

* **Corresponding author Jatinder Kaur:** Rukmini Devi Institute of Advanced Studies, Affilated to GGSIPU, New Delhi, India; E-mail: jeetu.jazz@gmail.com

Sandeep Kumar Kautish & Anuj Sheopuri (Eds.)

INTRODUCTION

The core of human resource management is maximizing the efficient use of people to achieve both business goals and personal aspirations. Its primary responsibilities encompass recruitment, administration, and exit-related functions within an organization. To sustain employee engagement and enhance productivity, HR professionals assess employee performance and orchestrate tailor-made training initiatives. The inception of HR as a distinct discipline emerged in the early 20th century, influenced by the ideas of Frederick Winslow Taylor (1856–1915). The terminology "human resource" was first coined by John R. Commons, an American institutional economist, in his 1893 publication "The Distribution of Wealth". Formal HR departments, created to handle the complex interactions between employers and employees, did not emerge until the 20th century. Performance management, a crucial component of human resources, is an ongoing conversation between managers and workers with the goal of attaining corporate goals and fostering employee skill development. This ongoing interaction encompasses delineating precise expectations, setting objectives, providing incessant feedback, and evaluating outcomes. Through recital management, a strong line of statements between managers and staff develops over the course of a year to achieve both organizational and personal objectives. To comprehend employee performance comprehensively, managers analyze the amassed data, addressing performance gaps with insights derived from the information. This process incorporates a range of tools, including the utilization of HR analytics.

Concept of HR Analytics

HR analytics is a process that involves gathering and using talent-related data in order to maximize key workforce capabilities. It serves as a decision-making tool harnessing available data to predict employee turnover, identify high-performing individuals, and forecast skill areas necessitating enhancement. Often referred to as people analytics, HR analytics empowers organizations to assess the influence of HR metrics on overall business performance, thereby facilitating data-driven decision-making. This approach enables organizations to make informed choices based on tangible data insights.

Literature Review

Dr. P. Raghunadha Reddy and P. Lakshmi Keerthi (2017) emphasize the crucial value of human resources within organizations. They promote an evidence-based strategy as the best method for making decisions, emphasizing how HR analytics not only supports this strategy but also pushes businesses to keep good data to support the return on investment of HR expenditures.

Anshu Sharma and Tanuja Sharma (2017), in their study article, "HR Analytics and Performance Appraisal System: A Conceptual Framework for Employee Performance Improvement", describe the influence of HR analytics on performance assessment systems and how this affects employees' incentive to improve their performance. According to their conceptual approach, the use of capable data scrutiny tools in HRA improves the accuracy of the evaluation process. Additionally, they offer perceptions for additional investigation into the field of performance management, offering prospective routes for development.

R. Anita and Dr. N. Sumathi (2019) investigate how employee performance is impacted by performance management systems. Based on the WERS 2004 dataset, they examine the dynamics of the link between enactment management systems and employee enactment. The study's goals include studying the performance management system, examining how it relates to employee performance, and eventually coming up with suggestions on how to best balance these elements.

Udhay Kailash and M Prathyusha (2020) contribute to the discourse with their research paper "HR Analytics: Methodical Measurement of HR Processes". They emphasize the use of HR analytics in assessing employee contributions to firms, forecasting workforce needs, and coordinating workforce usage with strategic objectives to improve overall business success. Their study focuses on the pharmaceutical industry, proposing a replicable HR analytics model for similar organizations within the sector and beyond.

H.H.D.P.J. Opatha (2020), in their research paper titled "HR Analytics: A Literature Review and New Conceptual Model", expounds on how HR analytics offers a data-driven framework for addressing workforce challenges through the synthesis of data using statistical models and specialized software. This approach facilitates nuanced decision-making and equips managers with insights to optimize human resource management practices.

Dr. Filza Hameed *et al.* (2021) underscore the importance of a dynamic and continuous performance management system. They advocate for addressing employee concerns collaboratively, creating a unified team atmosphere. The researchers recommend implementing acknowledgment methods to enhance motivation and engagement, fostering a sense of recognition. Involving employees in goal-setting and rewarding their efforts aligns their endeavors with organizational objectives.

Steven McCartney and Na Fu (2022) contribute to the discourse with their research paper titled "Bridging the Gap: Why, How, and When HR Analytics Can Impact Organizational Performance". They examine the potential of HR analytics to improve decision-making and accomplish corporate objectives while acknowledging the dynamic character of the field. In their paper, they offer a chain model that describes how HR skills make HRA possible, which then helps in evidence-based supervision and, finally, boosts administrative performance. This model emphasizes the transformative impact of HR analytics on organizational outcomes.

These research papers collectively underscore the growing importance of HRA in strategic decision-making, performance enhancement, and employee management across diverse sectors and industries.

Research Methodology

The research methodology employed in this study delineates the approach by which the research will be carried out. This encompasses the strategies for data collection, utilization of statistical analysis techniques, observational methodologies, and more. The pivotal role of research methodologies lies in substantiating and bolstering the chosen data collection methods and the core tenets of the research. In essence, research methodologies serve as the foundation that reinforces and complements the selected data collection approaches and pivotal aspects of the study. By adopting a rigorous methodology, the research aims to ensure the credibility and reliability of its findings while effectively addressing the research objectives.

Secondary Data

Evidence that has been collected from earlier research efforts rather than being collected directly by the researcher is secondary data. In essence, secondary data constitutes pre-existing data that has been compiled and stored by individuals or organizations for their respective purposes. In the context of this paper, secondary data is drawn from various sources, including websites and journals, to fulfill the research requirements. By utilizing secondary data, researchers leverage information that has already been processed and documented by others. This approach offers several advantages, such as time efficiency and the ability to analyze a broader range of perspectives and cases. The diverse collection of cases presented in this paper has been culled from a variety of reputable sources, allowing for a comprehensive examination of the subject matter while saving time and resources.

Purposes of the Study

1. To comprehend the role of HR analytics in enhancing performance management.

2. To state the advantages and obstacles to HR analytics incorporation.

Types of HR Analytics

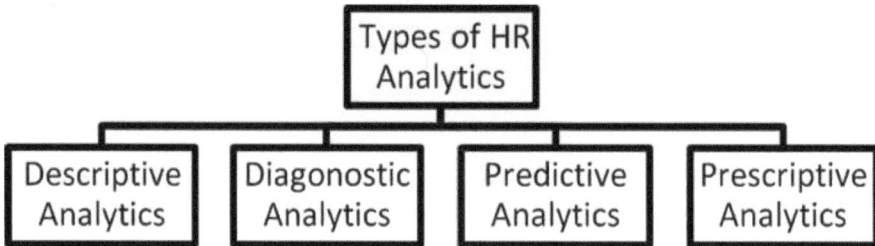

Fig. (1). Types of HR Analytics.
Source: Concept of HR Analytics.

Descriptive Analytics

The accumulation of raw data in its unprocessed state might lack significance, yet once structured and organized systematically, it becomes a valuable resource. Descriptive analytics, often referred to as observation and reporting, represents the foundational layer of analytical processes commonly employed for its fundamental insights. This methodology involves collating historical data and presenting it in a *COMPREHENSIBLE* format. For instance, descriptive analytics may be used to create a headcount report of all the employees in a company or a certain department. Furthermore, even more intricate metrics like turnover rates find their place under this category. Descriptive analytics revolves around scrutinizing past data to elucidate and interpret occurrences.

Diagnostic Analytics

While descriptive analytics illuminates the "what" behind events, diagnostic analytics delves into the "why". It transcends the realm of understanding occurrences and delves into the underlying causative factors. This phase involves transitioning from mere observation to an investigative approach that identifies patterns uncovered through the descriptive analysis and subsequently delves into their origins. Diagnostic analytics employs an array of techniques, including data drilling and data mining. These methods are instrumental in probing the foundational causes of issues and seeking viable solutions. Organizations that aspire to comprehend the underlying reasons for challenges must engage in diagnostic analytics, unraveling the complexities that drive problematic situations.

Predictive Analytics

While descriptive analytics centers on historical data and retrospective insights, predictive analytics shifts its focus toward the future. This form of analysis employs diverse statistical models and forecasts to anticipate forthcoming events. The central objective of predictive analytics is to uncover the organizational needs that lie ahead. These models are constructed upon the patterns and trends unearthed through descriptive analytics. For instance, predictive analytics could offer insights into the probable duration an employee might remain with the organization. It can also aid talent acquisition teams in assessing an employee's compatibility with the organizational culture.

Prescriptive Analytics

Once future scenarios have been predicted, the next logical query pertains to actionable steps. Prescriptive analytics serves as the vanguard in this regard, offering informed recommendations based on predictions and historical data. This type of analysis proves particularly advantageous for organizations contending with cyclical or seasonal demand fluctuations. For instance, a retailer might seek to ascertain the appropriate staffing levels during the holiday season. Moreover, prescriptive analytics can assist in strategically hiring new employees by aligning their skillsets and knowledge with the organization's requirements across the employee life cycle. This level of analysis assimilates insights gleaned from preceding tiers to prescribe precise courses of action. It harnesses the inherent potential of data to guide future decision-making. In contemporary organizations, various sophisticated HR analytical tools are wielded to facilitate these insights. Prominent examples include Visier, Tableau, QLIK, SPSS, and Microsoft Excel. These tools enable organizations to derive invaluable insights from data, thereby fostering more informed and strategic HR decision-making.

HR Analytics Tools

R - Programming

As a superior tool for analyzing and displaying huge quantities of data, R is comparable to Python. You can work with big datasets with this HR Analytics software. Even data sets with millions of rows may be cleaned with R. Studio, which is the most commonly used R IDE (Integrated Development Environments), followed by numbly.

Excel

Everyone already uses Excel to some degree. When using Excel, load the 'Analysis ToolPak'. Understanding Excel functions will allow doing critical data manipulations with ease. In addition, Excel offers a wide range of options for data visualization. When it comes to summarizing information, summary statistics may be of great use.

Tableau

For data aggregation from multiple sources, Tableau is one of the most popular business intelligence applications. Using easy-to-understand charts and graphs, the data is presented in a way that anybody can grasp. In addition, it is compatible with the cloud and offers real-time data analytics.

Python

Data Scientists choose Python because it is easy to learn. For statistical analysis of human resource data, it is a useful HR analytics tool. A number of free, open-source integrated development environments (IDEs) are available, including PyCharm and Spyder.

Power BI

The combination of Excel sheets, SQL databases, or Machine Learning APIs form Power BI (business intelligence) as a workforce analytics tool. It is possible to incorporate data from all of these different sources into Power BI. Using Power BI's dash-boarding capabilities, the aggregated data may be turned into an HR dashboard for reporting and data visualization. These include Power BI Pro and Premium, as well as the free version of Power BI.

Visier

When it comes to people data, Visier is an all-in-one solution that provides actionable insights. Business intelligence (BI) may link to different HR systems and combine them into one tool. For example, Visier utilizes algorithms to anticipate employee departures and internal movements, as well as promotions and other career advancements. Additionally, it may reveal distinct patterns in workforce data to assist in understanding how productivity and performance are influenced by certain approaches and techniques.

Benefits of HR Analytics

Lower Employee Turnover

Companies may be able to select better candidates and successfully lower their employee turnover rates if they use more data to inform their hiring decisions. Companies with low turnover rates can develop a vibrant, positive workplace culture, lower workplace errors, and facilitate new hire integration.

Making the Hiring Process More Effective

It speeds up the boarding of both HR and new hires, which saves the company time and money. The organization uses historical data that it has gathered over time to identify trends that are favorable in the hiring process so that it can concentrate resources on those trends and reduce problems.

Improving Training

By compiling HR data, the business can review its training procedure in order to learn what strategies work best for better supporting new hires and identify which practices or strategies it can drop. A new employee must pay close attention during the initial training process because it outlines their job duties and place in the company. The business can develop a better training process to better prepare new hires for success in their positions with a more thorough training program based on encouraging historical trends.

Effective Hiring

Effective hiring and training can assist new hires in adopting a positive attitude toward the organization and its culture. The willingness of new hires to participate in company culture and find their place within the company may increase if they feel more welcomed or confident in their skills.

Gaining Additional Employee Insights

HR analytics also assist companies in obtaining better, more detailed insights from their workforce. Employees frequently have a thorough understanding of the internal workings of the company, and they can provide better insight into the difficulties and strengths of the company.

Supporting Increased Productivity at Work

Businesses may profit from an increase in workplace productivity if better hiring decisions are driven by more data and a supportive corporate culture. Employees who are content and contented might be more eager to contribute ideas and work to the company, which would boost motivation and output.

Metrics Monitored by HR Analytics

Efficiency of Training

Determined through the analysis of a variety of data points, including performance enhancement, test results, and an increase in employees' roles within the company following training. To assess a training program's efficacy, measuring training efficiency can be essential.

Risk to Human Capital

This can include employee-related risks like the inability to find candidates with the necessary skills for a new type of job, the scarcity of qualified candidates for leadership roles, the possibility that an employee will leave the company for a variety of reasons like their relationship with managers, pay, or the absence of a clear succession plan. HR analytics may be used to measure each of these KPIs.

Offer Acceptance Rate

The percentage of formal employment offers that were accepted over all verbal job offers made over a certain time period is known as the offer acceptance rate. A greater proportion—more than 85%—indicates a good ratio. This information can be cast off to change the company's capacity-gaining strategy if it is lower.

Absenteeism

By separating the total number of scheduled workdays by the total quantity of days missed, the productivity measure of absenteeism is determined. Absenteeism may be an indication of contentment and can provide insight into a worker's general health.

Employee Training Expenses

Are calculated by dividing the entire cost of the program by the number of participants. The training's return on investment may be determined by evaluating its efficacy. You might want to reevaluate the expense of staff training if productivity is poor.

Revenue Per Employee

By dividing a company's income by the total number of employees, revenue per employee is determined. This illustrates the usual income generated by each employee. It serves as a benchmark for how well a company supports employee-based income production.

Obstacles to Implementing HR Analytics

Most organizations engage in the collection of employee data, which then fuels their efforts to strategize and reshape their business framework. However, the management of HR data within a company is far from a straightforward endeavor. The integration of analytics into HR operations has significantly streamlined the responsibilities of HR professionals over time. Analytics, in this context, empowers organizations to gain profound insights and swiftly model the correlations between employee trends and their impact on sales and profitability. Nonetheless, several obstacles stand in the way of organizations fully realizing the potential of people analytics.

Data Quality Challenge

HR analytics confronts a data quality predicament due to the vast quantities of data that are often complex to collect, generate, and store. The data amassed might contain missing or erroneous attributes, often stemming from inaccuracies in the information provided by employees. Instances of duplicated data or data corruption during transfer between sources are also common. The efficacy of HR analytics tools hinges on the availability of reliable data. When data quality issues arise, the outcomes generated might not align with expectations.

Data Governance Issue

The concept of data governance is often lacking when organizations engage with HR analytics tools. Data governance involves ensuring the ethical and lawful utilization of data. This principle dictates that the data harnessed by companies should be employed ethically and within legal boundaries. The utilization of HR analytics tools can complicate data management, as modern methodologies and techniques are employed to collect and interpret extensive datasets, subsequently driving data-informed decisions.

Deficiency in Data Analysis Skills

Despite companies actively advocating for the integration of analytics into HR functions, the reality remains that a shortage of analytical skills persists. While the adoption of analytics is promoted, a skills gap becomes evident when attempting to employ sophisticated analytical techniques. These skills gaps can hinder the successful implementation of analytics-driven HR strategies and initiatives.

Insufficient IT Resources

The implementation of analytics within HR demands a substantial investment in IT resources. Many organizations, particularly smaller ones, may lack the necessary infrastructure to establish a robust analytics program. Constructing the required technological framework can be both financially and temporally taxing. This financial constraint often dissuades organizations from venturing into HR analytics implementation.

Diverse Data Landscape

The realm of HR encompasses a diverse array of tools catering to various services, often sourced from different providers. However, these tools frequently operate in isolation, posing a significant hurdle for organizations aiming to leverage people analytics effectively. The challenge lies in integrating these disparate systems, a formidable task in itself.

Employee Resistance

Organizations face critiques from HR professionals who assert that the reliance on computers for HR functions, especially in areas like recruitment, diminishes the "human" aspect of "human resources". Concerns emerge that the analytical approach supersedes the personal touch. Moreover, the inherent limitations of analytical systems can lead to inaccuracies, potentially leading to skepticism about their predictive capabilities.

CONCLUSION

The imperative for organizations to address the question of employee retention prompts the utilization of HR analytics. This analytical method makes it possible to identify the demands and weaknesses of an employee, which facilitates the development of customized systems or programs aimed at improving recital and holding rates. Prominent organizations like Google use HRA to gather information on employee recitals, which helps identify the best training databases for both high- and low-accomplishment staff. Unfortunately, many businesses continue to ignore HR analytics and other related but underutilized organizational strategies. This study, however, focuses on harnessing HR practices to effect a transformation from traditional roles to transformative roles within organizations. The research endeavors to delve into and grasp the evolving role of analytics within the contemporary era. The growing demand for enhanced performance has positioned HR analytics as a pivotal tool for sculpting an innovative and competitive work environment.

Effectively executing this role necessitates substantial support for HR managers and leaders from their organizational counterparts. Their involvement requires an in-depth understanding of prevailing challenges. Changes in organization paradigms, leadership expansion, recruitment concerns, metrics evaluation, and HRA are just a few of the problems that these challenges cover. Leveraging the expertise of these domains, organizations can dissect complex situations and devise viable solutions to address these multifaceted problems.

REFERENCES

Anshu Sharma, Tanuja Sharma, (2017), HR analytics and performance appraisal system: A conceptual framework for employee performance improvement *Management Research Review, 40*(6).

Dr. P. Raghunadha Reddy, P. Lakshmi Keerthi (2017), HR Analytics' - An Effective Evidence Based HRM Tool *International Journal of Business and Management Invention, 6*(7).

H.H.D.P.J. Opatha (2020), HR Analytics: A Literature Review and New Conceptual Model *International Journal of Scientific and Research Publications, 10*(6).

Kale, Hritik & Anute, Nilesh. (2022). HR Analytics and its Impact on Organizations Performance. *International Journal of Research and Analytical Reviews, 9*(3), 619.

Muhammad Said, Dr. Imran Khan, Dr.Filza Hameed (2021), The impact of performance management system on employees' performance *International Journal of Business and Management Sciences, 2.*

Preeti Singhwal and Dr Neha VashisthaInternational (2023), HR Analytics and its Impact on Organizations Efficiency *Journal of Advances in Engineering and Management (IJAEM), 5*(4), 641-647. Available from: www.ijaem.net

R. Anita. Dr. N. Sumathi (2019), A study on the measuring the factors of HR analytics on performances management in services sector of selected companies in Chennai *JAC: A Journal of Composition Theory, 12*(12).

Steven McCartney and Na Fu (2022), Bridging the gap: why, how and when HR analytics can impact organizational performance *Management Decision, 68*(13).

Udhay Kailash and M Prathyusha (2020), HR Analytics Methodical Measurement of HR Processes *International Journal of Innovative Science and Research Technology, 5*(11).

SUBJECT INDEX

A

Absenteeism, reduced 36
Advancements, technological 70, 76, 133
AI-powered automation 54
Algorithms, predictive 100
Amalgamation 113, 117, 131
Analytical 9, 27, 55, 67, 97, 133, 138, 142
   skills 9, 55, 67, 97, 142
   tools 27, 133, 138
Analytics 24, 27, 37, 57, 78, 112
  human resource 24, 27, 37, 57, 112
  labor force 78
Analyze 89, 90
   compensation data 89
   industry trends and business forecasts 90
   survey data and feedback 89
Analyzing 32, 33, 34, 68, 77
   applicant data 68
   employee data 32, 33, 34
   employee skills 77
Asset acquisition 37
Attrition 12, 18, 38, 50, 63, 89, 125, 129
  customer 38
  risk prediction 89
Auditing processes 93

B

Building on descriptive analytics 59
Business 4, 13, 17, 25, 26, 32, 38, 39, 63, 82, 89, 90, 114, 118, 123, 134, 139, 142
  analyst 123
  ecosystem 17
  forecasts 90
  framework 142
  intelligence (BI) 139
  leaders 13, 32
  market 118
  outcomes 4, 25, 89, 114
  performance 4, 26, 39, 134
  processes 38
  strategies 63, 82
Business landscape 34, 38, 55, 59, 60, 72, 85, 97
  competitive 60
  dynamic 34, 55
  fast-developing 59
  growing 72

C

Candidate(s) 42, 43, 75, 127, 141
  qualified 42, 43, 141
  qualitative 127
  selection 75
Capabilities, analytical 55
Career 96, 104
  development plans 96
  growth opportunities 104
Commitment, organizational 66
Communication skills 54
Company performance 67
Compensation packages 63
Compliance manager 8
Cost management 45
Criminal records 47
Crises, global 61
Crisis situation 34
Cultural fit assessment 88
Culture 2, 8, 27, 33, 35, 52, 61, 74, 77, 87, 98, 101, 105, 106, 140
  company's 27, 52, 106
  innovative working 2
  positive workplace 140
  supportive corporate 140

D

Data 19, 26, 50, 67, 69, 75, 79, 81, 105, 136, 137, 142
  analysis tools 75
  collection and management 105
  collection methods 136

consolidation 19
corruption 142
dashboards 69
drilling 26, 137
governance issue 142
infrastructure 67
integration 50, 79
mining 26, 137
storage 67
transformation 81
validation 81
warehouse 50
Data visualization 45, 51, 72, 80, 83, 139
  techniques 45, 51
  tools and dashboards transform 80
Decision-making-oriented approach 113
Deficiency in data analysis skills 142
Deloitte survey report 19
Diverse data landscape 143
Drive 15, 70, 97
  efficiency 15
  employee engagement 97
  innovation 70
Driving force 97
Duplicated 82, 142
  data 142
  entries 82

E

Economic 3, 37, 116
  benchmarks, external 3, 116
  indicators, positive 37
Ecosystem, organization/delivery 12
Effective 77, 87, 105, 140
  hiring 140
  succession planning 87, 105
  team composition 77
Efficiency 45, 50, 52, 55, 62, 64, 109, 113,
    115, 130, 131, 141
  maintaining cost 64
  measuring training 141
Emotional intelligence 32, 33
Empirical analysis 133
Employee(s) 12, 18, 26, 28, 31, 32, 33, 34, 37,
    44, 45, 49, 51, 58, 61, 64, 65, 66, 67, 69,
    68, 70, 73, 75, 76, 78, 79, 80, 81, 86, 88,
    90, 91, 93, 98, 100, 101, 103, 104, 105,
    108, 109, 110, 133, 134, 135, 142, 143
  aspirations 86

attrition 28, 133
-based income production 142
behaviors 31, 133
commitment 65
data 32, 75, 80, 91, 98, 108, 109, 142
demographics 100
development programs 33
empowerment 93
feedback 31, 68, 101
growth 65
high-performing 49, 51, 67
high-potential 69, 70, 90
hiring 103, 104
networks 34
onboarded 88
onboarding and integration 88
performance 58, 61, 64, 65, 100, 101, 103,
    104, 105, 109, 110, 134, 135
privacy 100
productivity 61, 133
profiles 18
programs 68
records 78, 79, 81
resistance 143
retention 37, 44, 45, 61, 73, 76, 143
skills 66, 108
surveys 78, 81
turnover 12, 26, 44, 45, 133, 134
Employee engagement 36, 57, 58, 60, 63, 65,
    68, 70, 72, 76, 77, 83, 84, 85, 86
  efforts 68,
  enhancement 86
  initiatives 65
  survey data 63
Environment 29, 58, 62
  competitive business 58
Era, digital 97
Ethical and inclusive practices 74, 76
Expenses 30, 125
  labor 30
  technological 125

F

Financial constraint 143
Forecast 63, 69
  employee turnover 63
  turnover risks 69

G

General data protection regulation (GDPR) 46, 93
Global business services (GBS) 16
Growth 2, 29, 61, 75, 97, 98, 100, 112, 117
  earnings 29
  factor 2

H

Health 13, 70, 93
  insurance portability and accountability act (HIPAA) 93
  mental 70
  occupational 13
Hiring 35, 43, 44, 45, 52, 53, 67, 103, 105, 106, 107, 108, 112, 114, 119, 121, 122, 123, 125, 129, 131, 140
  analytics 119
  individual 125
  practices 45, 52
  process 35, 43, 44, 45, 53, 67, 103, 105, 106, 108, 140
  qualitative 119, 131
HR 67, 73, 75, 80
  information systems (HRIS) 67, 75
  -related data 73, 80
Human capital 3, 8, 14, 15, 30, 31, 34, 36, 37, 39, 40, 112
  investments 8, 112
  management (HCM) 3, 14, 15, 30, 31, 34, 36, 37, 39, 40
Human resource(s) 1, 2, 3, 7, 15, 16, 20, 24, 26, 43, 57, 58, 59, 62, 72, 73, 74, 76, 78, 85, 97, 101, 112, 116, 134, 139
  business partner (HRBPs) 16
  data 139
  management (HRM) 3, 7, 24, 43, 59, 62, 78, 85, 97, 101, 134
  manager 120
  managing 1
  shared services (HRSS) 15, 16

I

IBM 15
  planning analytics 15
  system 15

Industries, pharmaceutical 15, 135
Industry trends, emerging 70
Information technology-enabled services (ITeS) 2
Integrated development environments (IDEs) 138, 139
Internal recruitment costs 125

J

Job 44, 45, 68, 76, 104, 120
  application form 120
  satisfaction 44, 45, 68, 76, 104

L

Landscape 34, 39, 74, 84, 94, 101, 133
  competitive market 34
  contemporary 133
Laws, labor 48
Leadership development 13, 40, 90
Learning 13, 35, 58, 65, 74, 80, 89, 114, 116, 118, 125, 130
  computer-based 35

M

Machine learning 33, 38, 49, 54, 59, 69, 70, 76, 95, 98, 101, 107, 108, 109
  algorithms 33, 59, 95, 108
  integration 69
  techniques 107, 109
Management 13, 37
  asset 37
  career 13
Management system 13
  artificial intelligence-based human resource 13
Memorandum of understanding (MoU) 14
Monitor workforce trends 69

N

National association of software companies (NASSCOM) 2
Natural language processing (NLP) 60, 96
Network analysis 38
Neural networks 102, 107

O

Onboarding programs 88
Oracle HCM cloud 13

P

People management 58, 62, 72, 74, 76, 94
  businesses approach 74
  contemporary 58
  organizations approach 62, 76
  policies 72
  revolutionize 94
Performance 1, 12, 17, 18, 67, 135
  appraisal system 135
  management system (PMS) 1, 12, 17, 18,
    67, 135
Power, transformative 98
Programs 89, 143
  robust analytics 143
  tailor learning 89

R

Risk, employee-related 141

S

Salary negotiations 52, 118
Skill 33, 74, 76, 86, 90, 97, 98
  demands 86, 90
  development 33, 74, 76, 97, 98
  requirements 76, 90
Social media 44, 49, 54
  analytics 54
  platforms 44
  profiles 54
  Recruitment 49
Soft skills 32, 33
Software 2, 67
  business 2
Sourcing 120, 121, 127
  agent 121
  channel effectiveness 120, 127
SQL databases 139
Succession planning strategy 108
Sustain employee engagement 134
Systemic people analytics (SPA) 2

T

Tailored development plans 108
Talent management (TM) 2, 13, 33, 34, 107,
    108, 109, 112, 113, 114, 116, 117, 118,
    130, 131
Tata consultancy services (TCS) 13
Technical skills 47, 108
Techniques 26, 78, 102, 108, 137, 139, 142
  cross-validation 102, 18
Technology 13, 75, 7
  cognitive 13
  digital 75
  emerging 76
Training 65, 66, 75, 79, 84, 97, 108, 134, 140
  initiatives 66, 75, 134
  programs 65, 84, 97, 140
  records 79, 10
Transaction work 16
Transactional 16, 97
  processes 97
  work 16
Transformational field 59
Transformative 62, 71, 109
  approach 109
  force 62, 71
Turnover 26, 32, 33, 36, 43, 50, 58, 61, 68, 73,
    75, 76, 79, 86, 90, 104, 108, 118, 137
  analysis 90
  costs 104
  high 61
  rates 58, 68, 75, 76, 79, 137
  reduced 36, 43, 108

U

Utilization, lawful 142

V

Video 53, 54
  and social media analytics 54
  screenings 53
Visibility, complete 15

W

Wage fixation 7
Walk-in interviews 121

Wellness, improving employee 70
Work environments 24, 27, 32, 52, 144
  competitive 144
  dynamic 32
Work from 8
  anywhere (WFA) 8
  home (WFH) 8
  office (WFO) 8
Work-life balance 61, 70, 76
  ensuring 61
Workforce 3, 4, 13, 27, 32, 33, 34, 37, 39, 54,
      57, 58, 59, 60, 61, 63, 64, 68, 71, 72, 73,
      74, 78, 79, 80, 83, 85, 86, 87, 96, 97, 98,
      100, 135, 139
  analytics 3, 4, 13, 27, 39, 68
  analytics tool 139
  data 61, 73, 139
  diversity 37
  dynamics 71, 78, 84
  engaged 34
  engagement 13
  forecasting 135
  landscape 78
  management 32, 33, 80, 83, 85
  productivity 72, 86
  strategy 63
  success 54
  trends 57, 78, 79, 96
Workforce planning 15, 34, 57, 58, 60, 61, 63,
      68, 72, 74, 90, 96
  and succession management 63
  proactive 74
  software 15
Workplace(s) 35, 69, 72, 78, 87, 90, 98, 100,
     140
  inclusive 69, 87, 90
  modern 72
  productivity 140

www.ingramcontent.com/pod-product-compliance
Lightning Source LLC
Chambersburg PA
CBHW041443210326
41599CB00004B/113